ADVANCE PRAISE

A manager I was working with was excited in the hope to finally get the promotion he thought he deserved. He thought he had everything lined up to gain his promotion into the executive ranks—from achieving clear results to having the support of his immediate manager. Unfortunately, and unbeknownst to him, another leader above him blocked his promotion because of a past conflict the two of them had. It took him a long time to recover from this setback, and also cost his company the loss of his motivation and discretionary effort. Getting promoted is a major milestone in one's career. It's important! That's why Manbir Kaur's book *Get Your Next Promotion* is so critical. Every leader, manager, ambitious professional and anyone involved in human resources should read it and share it. It breaks down exactly what you need to know to think strategically about your career and accelerate your success. Add it to your must-read list.

Andrew Neitlich, *Director, Center for Executive Coaching, United States*

Every hardworking and ambitious young professional dreams of bagging a leadership role. Manbir shares stories of experienced corporate leaders and articulates in very simple terms a step-by-step approach to get there through the right career moves and soft skills development. A great read especially for those at crossroads in their jobs, deciding which path is right for them.

Nayana Mitter, *Associate Partner, Ernst and Young*

What a book Manbir has written for all corporate employees! The topics covered are pertinent, ranging from core learning and development to career planning, emotional intelligence and blind spots which are critical for any employee to manage and master. The narrative is lucid and striking with practical suggestions. This will be a great companion for all corporate employees.

Vishal Dua, *Regional Financial Director,*
Asia-Pacific (APAC), TAG

Manbir's book *Get Your Next Promotion* takes the readers on a step-by-step approach in their career growth right from goal setting to meaningful conversations to personal branding to big picture. She has articulated very well how professional success is important for each one to achieve their dreams backed by some interesting stories.

I personally recommend this book to my sales fraternity for their next promotion with the right emotion.

Anil Menghani, *GM & Vice President—Asia, Pacific,*
Japan and China (APJC), CleverTap

How to get the next promotion is a question that comes up often in my coaching conversations with professionals in corporations. Manbir writes with clarity and honesty about a subject that leads to frustrations and resignations in many organizations. You will finally understand why, sometimes, others are chosen instead of you and what can you do to get ready for the next promotion.

Steliana van de Rijt-Economu, *Founder, Leadership*
Coach and Author of Mothers as Leaders

In today's dynamic business environment, talent provides limitless possibilities. The 'rope' to ascend in the career path for such talents is always available but one needs to be smart, not to hang oneself (with the rope) in sheer passion, instead of climbing up to the top. While one's own effort may help get a better grip on the 'rope', the eclectic collection of the most enriching experience from the top global leaders in form of stories in this book makes it perhaps the most unique book which will help the talents exponentially accelerate their professional progressions...and climb the rope...a must read.

Manish Oberoi, *Senior Telecom Leader*

MANBIR KAUR

Los Angeles | London | New Delhi
Singapore | Washington DC | Melbourne

First published in 2020 by

SAGE Publications India Pvt. Ltd
B1/I-1 Mohan Cooperative Industrial Area
Mathura Road, New Delhi 110 044, India
www.sagepub.in

SAGE Publications Inc
2455 Teller Road
Thousand Oaks, California 91320, USA

SAGE Publications Ltd
1 Oliver's Yard, 55 City Road
London EC1Y 1SP, United Kingdom

SAGE Publications Asia-Pacific Pte Ltd
18 Cross Street #10-10/11/12
China Square Central
Singapore 048423

Published by Vivek Mehra for SAGE Publications India Pvt. Ltd. Typeset in 11/14 pt Baskerville by Fidus Design Pvt. Ltd, Chandigarh.

Library of Congress Cataloging-in-Publication Data Available

ISBN: 978-93-5388-477-2 (PB)

SAGE Team: Neha Pal, Neena Ganjoo, Parul Prasad and Rajinder Kaur

*To the power of
free will bestowed
on all of us!*

Thank you for choosing a SAGE product!
If you have any comment, observation or feedback,
I would like to personally hear from you.

Please write to me at **contactceo@sagepub.in**

Vivek Mehra, Managing Director and CEO, SAGE India.

Bulk Sales

SAGE India offers special discounts
for purchase of books in bulk.
We also make available special imprints
and excerpts from our books on demand.

For orders and enquiries, write to us at

Marketing Department
SAGE Publications India Pvt Ltd
B1/I-1, Mohan Cooperative Industrial Area
Mathura Road, Post Bag 7
New Delhi 110044, India

E-mail us at **marketing@sagepub.in**

Subscribe to our mailing list
Write to **marketing@sagepub.in**

This book is also available as an e-book.

CONTENTS

FOREWORD

I relaunched my business at the age of 55, back in 2011, after 15 years in the corporate world. It was always my calling, and I have been thinking about leadership for many years before that, in fact, I wrote my first book, *Success Yourself*, in 1996. In 2010, my leadership assessment model appealed to Steve Jobs and that became my first big assignment back then. I enjoyed working with him as his executive coach and with many great leaders and coaches ever since.

I believe that we have a massive leadership gap; there are not many leaders who are willing to push themselves to become a role model. I am working hard to make a difference, and my latest book, *The Intelligent Leader*, is my way of giving back to the world. While every day I strive to make the world a better place (one leader, one coach at a time), my book aims to help leaders that I cannot personally connect with.

Manbir is a fellow coach with similar goals. She has been working as an Executive Coach for about a decade now. She has through her first book *Are You The Leader You Want To Be?* shared a unique framework (HUMAN Leadership) to help leaders in technology organizations build great teams that can perform even under duress. She has a noble vision of helping leaders, across the world, become better at what they do.

In this book, she has gone one step further and is now looking at the factors that stop people from getting into the leadership roles. As coaches, we believe in the inherent potential of people and work with them to make sure that they harness it.

She believes that despite having potential, some get stuck for various reasons. She rightly brings out that there is no single magic skill or strength that can take one to the leadership positions. To become a leader, one must master multiple facets and what better way than to learn the same from the stories of successful leaders! She has worked with 10 leaders, who come from different parts of the world, from different industries, each following a unique path to become a leader in their own reckoning. She has carefully brought out the importance of 10 key aspects in their success. While each leader's success is a result of multiple factors, she has curated the stories to highlight the importance of one specific aspect in each one of them. The smart readers can see that each story actually has more than one aspect, and that these aspects are all interlinked at a deeper level.

She has written *Get Your Next Promotion* in such a way that it becomes easy for the readers to relate to each aspect. The book will help readers to know what to look for and how to master one of the aspects before applying their energy on to the next one. As you progress through the book, they will come together like pieces of a puzzle that you always wanted to solve.

Are you looking to become a leader in your own right? You must begin the transformation now! Get ready to achieve your potential!

JOHN MATTONE

Bestselling author, the #1 authority on intelligent
leadership and the World's Top Executive Coach
(Former Coach to Steve Jobs)

ACKNOWLEDGEMENTS

Great leaders make the world a better place. Those who willingly make a gift of their time to help others grow make it a beautiful and a happy place too. Thank you everyone who nurtures others.

I will always be indebted to the awesome leaders who came forward to share their own stories through this book. The mentorship and knowledge you offer is an invaluable gift for the readers. Thank you Arindam Haldar, Malur Narayan, R. Mahalakshmi, Tapan Sahoo, Amandeep Gupta, Steve Alexander, Apurva Purohit, Kulmeet Bawa, Ravinder Dang and Ashley Passow for your openness and willingness to share your experiences so that others may learn valuable lessons from your career journey. This book may have remained just an idea without the candid and incredibly open conversations that you all had with me over this last one year. Please accept my immense gratitude.

I am eternally grateful to the three amazing men in my life. Thank you dad, for kindling a spirit of courage and building in me the deep desire to learn and grow, thanks my husband, Jatinder, for being with me through everything, thank you Ishnoor, my son, for being a patient listener and being my best friend. You have all encouraged me to carry on, even when things seemed tough.

A deep sense of gratitude to all my coaching clients; you all have been great teachers for me. Thank you for believing in me. Each of the deep conversations with you inspires me to do more.

To Kathy Mitchell, thank you for your constant encouragement and for all the great questions you ask. You know, you are my 'go-to' friend, in all those desperate times. Our friendship means a lot to me.

To all my Conversational Intelligence mastermind colleagues— Uli Mueller, Kathryn Goldman, Regina Huber, Iris Grimm and Yvonne Ryan—thanks for all those late evening calls that always ignite my thoughts and for the amazing learning experiences.

Thanks to all my friends who helped me become what I am today. To all my coach friends who have been with me on this amazing journey—JP Singh, Aditi Malhotra, Malveika Joshi, Anjana Chandra, Uttara Pattanaik, Avtar Singh, Saraswati Anand and Cindy Peace—thanks for your valuable time, suggestions and timely support in helping me to write this book.

Thanks to everyone at SAGE, who helped me so much. Special thanks to Neha and Manisha for their creative insights and for helping me evolve an Idea into a book that you have in your hands today.

1

PROMOTIONS ARE AN INTEGRAL PART OF WORK

❝ ❞

We keep moving forward, opening new doors, and doing new things because we're curious and curiosity keeps leading us down new paths.

WALT DISNEY

We always talk about moving forward. I believe that the notion of moving forward comes from 'time'. Time has only one direction, and if we are to keep pace with it, we must also keep on moving forward. I simply love what Walt Disney says about moving forward. We already know the past, and with our innate curiosity to see more, do more and experience more, we must look for new experiences in the future. This is all so fundamental to human nature.

If you can't fly then run, if you can't run then walk, if you can't walk then crawl, but whatever you do you have to keep moving forward.

Martin Luther King, Jr

Yes, we must keep moving forward. But how important is it?

We hate to feel like we are stuck in one place. After sometime, we stop enjoying even the most beautiful scenes and we want to move forward to the next adventure in our life. And even if we choose to stay at one place because of our limitations at that particular moment of time, I assure you that it is a good thing to be looking to the future with hope and goals instead of settling for the 'average experience'.

Another important aspect which fixes our directionality with respect to 'forward' is the fact about our growth. With time, we grow faster, smarter, bigger, more intelligent, wiser, more experienced, more responsible, wealthier and so on and on. So the growth is built into our mindset; if we do not get growth, we feel bad about it. Like Sam Waterston says, 'If you're not moving forward, you're falling back.'

PROMOTIONS ARE AN INTEGRAL PART OF WORK

Work is an essential part of our life and as such, the same rules of growth and moving forward apply to our professional life as well. If you find yourself stagnant at your place of work, you feel the need to do something about it!

Promotion is a natural way for growth. While sometimes promotion can be a very basic need, because it results into a much-needed salary raise, but quite a few times it can be at a much higher level of needs in Maslow's hierarchy.[1] For example, a promotion could tell the employee that he/she is needed by the organization and satisfy the need to 'belong'. Or it could even become a prestige issue and satisfy the need of 'self-esteem', and if the employee does not get promotion, it may result into poor morale and low engagement.

Professionals need to meet different requirements for promotion at different points of their career. This book deals with the most difficult scenario called 'the Plateau'. Many of you may encounter it on the journey to the top management and may get stuck. Depending on your organizational structure and your own unique situation, a plateau can come much earlier in your career. This will be discussed in more detail in the subsequent chapter. However, since this book deals with the most difficult scenario of all the scenarios, the strategies presented here will help readers at all the levels or stages.

CHARTING CAREER SUCCESS

Many brilliant professionals struggle with engineering their own career growth beyond the initial stages. If you are stuck, you may relate to some of the following statements:

- Career paths are not clear in the organization

- Nothing is clearly communicated regarding promotions

- The organization does not value the 'real' skills that form its backbone

- Look who got promoted while I am still waiting

- There does not seem to be an opportunity for me in the organization

- No one cares about me

Career paths are different, and everyone does not get the same opportunities. But one thing is very clear that everyone desires to make a difference, be valued, be recognized or be appreciated for excellence in something. No one sets out on their career path with a desire to be mediocre. Many people come to the realization, sooner or later that they are not quite there yet, and that they still have a lot of potential which is not being utilized due to the lack of opportunities.

A few people remain top contributors throughout their career, because they have found the secret sauce of the 'success' recipe; they somehow came to know about what is expected of them at various stages and how they can contribute at their best.

3

Dr Marshall Goldsmith's statement has a distinct ring of truth when he says, 'What got you here won't get you there'.[2] The truth is that if you want to be successful throughout your career, you must change the way you contribute to the organization.

Before we get to the part where I share with you some new tools, I would like to simplify the career growth and the struggle of getting stuck. In remaining part of this chapter, we will start by looking at the four stages of career development model. This will help you to relate to the direction that you must take to make career progress. In the next chapter, we will talk about the 'plateau' which will help you to analyse your situation if you are stuck and help you understand what might be holding you back. Without much ado, let us start with the four-stage model.

FOUR STAGES OF CAREER DEVELOPMENT

A model developed based on research by Dr Gene Dalton and Dr Paul Thompson explains the career growth in terms of individual contribution to the organization. Global Novations (later acquired by Korn Ferry) conducted multiple researches across the globe and presented some interesting reports on the same as well.[3]

The four stages of career based on this model are as below.

- *Contributing dependently:* This is in a way beginning of career, when you are under supervision. You define yourself as, 'I am a part of the XX team. We take care of YY.'

- *Contributing independently:* This is the next stage of your career, when you can perform a piece of work on your own. You define yourself as, 'I am a part of XX team. I personally take care of ZZ.'

- *Contributing through others:* This is the third stage of the career, when you start leading a team and are responsible for a function. You define yourself as, 'I lead XX team. Our team is responsible for YY.'

- *Contributing strategically:* This is the fourth stage of the career, when you start defining the direction for a specific part of the organization. You define yourself as, 'I lead XX function. This year we plan to do ABCD.'

In brief, as you move along the career path, your impact on the business keeps increasing. You derive much satisfaction from the increasing value of the work you do and the impact it has on the organization.

Let us look at these stages in a little more detail and see what the key characteristics of each of them are, so that you can gauge the difference in the performance requirements for each of the stages.

Stage 1: Contributing Dependently

Full of energy, enthusiasm and a sense that you can change the world. Leaders expect you to deliver based on the instructions. You are new, you have some great skills and you are good at what you do. You have ideas, but you do not know the complexity and intricacies of running businesses. You are also easily distracted. You are not expected to understand everything and are not yet considered worthy of 'the big picture'. Your loyalties are under evaluation, and you are being observed. At this stage, you are just 'tasked' and 'measured'. Your capability to learn fast, follow instructions, deliver on time and with good quality are key for success at this stage.

One young employee resigned, and this is what he said in the exit interview, '*This was my first year here and the experience has been very bad. I wanted to contribute a lot and had a lot of opinions. No one paid any heed to what I said or wanted to do. It was very frustrating.*' This is what his manager said to HR when confronted with the feedback, '*The employee was*

5

always questioning everything without trying to understand the whole picture. He does not have patience to listen and learn. To get him to do something was hard work. If he had started by delivering first and shown his value, I would have spared time to satisfy his curiosity.'

There can be serious mismatches in expectations if one is not careful.

If you are in this stage, you may be expected to do the following:

- Accept supervision and show willingness to follow

- Successfully complete the tasks given

- Apply your mind and be creative, but within the domain of 'defined scope'

- Deliver on time

- Deliver quality

- Have a willingness to learn 'the ways' of the business

- Learn quickly to repeat tasks once assigned

If you are dependable and are a quick study, your role and responsibilities will start increasing. You need to be in this stage long enough to start speaking the expected business language, learn the ropes and build a solid foundation. Once you are ready, you can then move on to the next stage. You must not stay far too long in this stage that you start to lose your value and become very easily replaceable.

Stage 2: Contributing Independently

You are dependable. You have proven yourself in delivering the assigned tasks over and over. You have started to understand the system and are now considered ready to take up a bigger responsibility.

You have a voice now and people listen to your suggestions and accept your expertise in a specific area. You have now carved out a space for yourself, and are responsible for a specific function, that is, a part of the process. You may not need guidance or supervision to complete the task that you own. You have developed working relationships with the people who interface with your work. You discuss and negotiate with them the timelines, deliverables and other details. You start realizing that being a team player is important and start understanding a bigger part of the overall picture. You learn about dependencies and cross-linkages.

You can now take decisions that just impact your own space. You are in control of your own time and are measured for the outcomes. You like the independence and may not seek much guidance in completing the task. In fact, you may hate when you are micromanaged. An employee with about four years of experience, resented being reminded of the things he already knew. He was happy when he moved to a new function and found his new manager gave him a lot of independence. He said, '*I love it here, I get to do my things and am considered accountable for the results. I am pushed to deliver more but I am given freedom to find my own path.*'

If you are in this stage, you may be expected to do the following:

- Assume full responsibility for a project or part thereof

- Work independently without much supervision

- Continue to develop technical expertise around your work area

- Develop a reputation

- Build relationships with relevant stakeholders

Majority of the workforce in any organization at any given point of time lies in this stage. This stage is also known as Individual Contributor. This stage is very critical to building the foundation for the career. You must spend enough time in this stage to gain expertise in at least one area of the work. You must still remember that you cannot always stay in this stage for one key reason; your expertise may lose importance at some point in time.

Stage 3: Contributing through Others

You do not need to be a people manager to contribute through others. Research done by Korn Ferry suggests that about one-third of the people in Stage 3 are non-supervisors. There are many roles that exist in which as an individual contributor you can still deliver through others.

In Stage 3, you are now ready to take responsibility for work done by others. There are many additional skills and capabilities that you need to be successful in Stage 3. Stage 3 is also the highest stage that most of us will ever reach. Korn Ferry research conducted during 2007–2010 suggests that only about 5 per cent of people reach Stage 4, so you may even be spending your lifetime in Stage 3.[4] Of all the stages, transition to Stage 3 is the toughest. There are many new skills that you need to learn, including delegation, appreciating and acknowledging the work done by others, balance between micromanagement and loss of control, mentoring and developing others, project management, time management, building relationships far and wide (within your organization as well as outside the organization), influencing, negotiations and so on.

One person in Stage 3 said, '*I worked hard to get this project sanctioned, I had to convince not just my manager but the other two cross-functional leaders. Now they have each nominated one person from their team and we are three people working together to drive the project. I thought it is my baby but realized that I need to work together to create success for the organization. Sometimes we have to go through tough negotiations, but the project is progressing fine.*'

If you are in Stage 3, you may be expected to do the following:

- Increase breadth of knowledge, unlike Stage 2, where you focus on depth and speciality

- Develop a broader sense of the business

- Inspire and motivate others

- Be the mentor, take active interest in developing others

- Be the face of the organization to the external world

- Build a network—internal as well as external

One of the key challenges that some of you face in Stage 3 is that most of your time goes into non-domain, people management work. A few people may still like to keep learning in their own domain area to remain an expert and enjoy the moments of independence. All others will learn to live in the world of interdependence.

Stage 4: Contributing Strategically

As per the research by Korn Ferry, only about 5 per cent of the people progress to this level of contribution and there will never be a place for more than a few, at the very top of the organization.[4] If you are in Stage 4, you are an experienced professional, and you help visualize the future and anticipate changes in the business environment and prepare the organization to deal with it. You lead the innovation and idea generation for new systems, processes and so on, that are needed to move the organization in new directions. Once the direction for future is set, you go about making the vision a reality. You are the face of the organization and you have to instil confidence in a wide set of stakeholders to assure the success of the organization.

Unlike previous stages, where most of your time goes into execution, in this stage your main job is to work with various stakeholders to create the strategy. You own the risk of going wrong and the responsibility to choose a certain direction even when things are not clear.

You are expected to do the following:

- Provide strategic direction to the organization

- Define critical business needs

- Drive critical business opportunities

- Make sure that the resources are available to carry out the initiatives

- Use your power in the best interests of the organization

- Prepare the next level of leadership

There are no limits as to what you can do, except as defined by you. Some leadership teams have taken their organizations to unimaginable heights just by the sheer will and a powerful vision, while others have brought the death blows to their organizations by taking some wrong steps. Look at the example of Nokia mobile phones. What went wrong with them? Did they not see Apple coming up with new models? Did they underestimate the power of touch phones? Were they late to react? Who would you hold responsible, the 95 per cent of staff that was in Stage 1 or 2 or 3? Or just the 5 per cent or lesser staff that was in Stage 4? Ultimately the final accountability lies with the leaders in Stage 4.

SEEKING PROMOTION

Now that you have looked at all the four stages of contribution, let us now look at what makes one stage bigger than the other, and that how does all of this relate to your promotion or growth.

The basic parameter is contribution. The four different stages have drastically different contribution levels.

Stage 1: The value you add is a fraction of your own contribution, because the results that you produce are based on the contribution by others.

Stage 2: The value you add is equal to the value you create by yourself.

Stage 3: The value you add is not just about your work anymore. It is a function of people you influence to deliver on the projects/functions you lead. So there is a multiplier effect; the more you influence, the higher will be your potential contribution.

Stage 4: The value you create increases exponentially compared to your own. You will now be influencing multiple Stage 3 leaders, each of them has a multiplier effect of their own. If you have the right Stage 3 leaders, you will be able to create 'magic'. Well, almost!

Coming back to the beginning, you have an innate desire to grow, to make a difference. With the contribution levels explained above, it is but natural to keep moving up the stages to make sure that you are able to influence a larger part of the organization and make a bigger difference. Promotion thus must be related to the change from one stage to another. Organizational titles may or may not be the right metric. Some promotions give you a bigger title or an increase in salary, while keeping your scope of work the same. Typically, Stage 3 is a big domain with various levels within this stage built-in to handle the size and diversity of functions within the organization and can be quite a maze for navigating your career.

There are different skills, capabilities and requirements for success at each stage and that is what makes you successful at one, but will not necessarily make you successful at the next. So, think again whether your success at one stage can be a solid claim to move into the next.

PREPARING FOR THE NEXT STAGE

There are no guarantees that you will succeed when you grow up to next stage. Your past is no prediction of the future. So why do you get promoted? And if others are chosen instead of you, why?

The main questions that this book will help you to answer are:

- How to be ready for the next stage?

- How to make sure that you are the best among equals?

The structure of the book is pretty simple. In the next chapter, we will cover the aspects which may hold you back. We will explore the key hurdles from the individual perspective and why does it all look so hazy. The rest of the book consists of 10 strategies that will help you to become ready for your next promotion. Each chapter is dedicated to sharing the experience of a leader on a specific strategy. By the end of the book, you will have a few potential options to explore. These will help you to unleash your full potential.

REFERENCES

1. Maslow A. *Maslow's hierarchy of needs*. Available from: https://en.wikipedia.org/wiki/Maslow%27s_hierarchy_of_needs [Accessed 10 February 2020].

2. Goldsmith M. *What got you here won't get you there*. Available from: https://www.marshallgoldsmith.com/product/book-2/ [Accessed 10 February 2020].

3. Dalton GW, Thompson PH, Price RL. The four stages of professional careers—a new look at performance by professionals. *Organizational Dynamics*. 1977;6(1): 19–42.

4. Ferry K. *The four stages of contribution*. Available from: https://www.kornferry.com/insights/articles/the-four-stages-of-contribution [Accessed 10 February 2020].

2

THE PLATEAU

66 99

A plateau is defined as the point in a career where the likelihood of additional hierarchical promotion is very low. Career plateaus are a natural consequence of the way the organizations are shaped. Since there are fewer positions than aspirants at each higher rung of the organizational ladder, virtually all managers reach positions from which further upward mobility is unlikely.

**THOMAS FERENCE, JAMES STONER
AND KIRBY WARREN**

In October 1977, Thomas Ference, James Stoner and Kirby Warren's seminal work first defined the career plateau. Their paper was published in the *Academy of Management Review* and was titled, 'Managing the Career Plateau'.[1]

The definition is quite accurate even today, because many Stage 3 people will find themselves in this situation sooner or later. Some Stage 2 people may also find themselves stuck at that level, though that may be because of different reasons. Lot of things have changed in the business environment, the organizations and the way the careers are built today. So, there are other aspects to be considered. But before we consider the changes and their application, let us explore in a little more detail the framework they presented at that time.

They called the person who reached the plateau as the 'Plateauee'. They acknowledged that the plateauee is the solid citizen of the organization and forms the bulk of the organization's strength, doing most of the work.

They further identified that there are two scenarios of plateauing.

- *Organizationally plateaued:* Generally, because of lack of available positions. Having the capability to perform but still not able to get a promotion. They further listed three sub-scenarios as given below:

  › *Competition:* There are more capable people for the same job, either internally or externally available.

  › *Age:* The organization sees value in training a younger person, who may have a longer productive career, rather than seeking replacements again and again.

  › *Organizational need:* These people may be too critical in their current roles to be considered for promotion. The organization may not be ready to absorb the loss of moving them to bigger roles as no effective replacement is available.

- *Personally plateaued:* Because the organization sees these people as lacking the capability or desire to perform the higher-level job. They further listed three sub-scenarios as given next:

  › *Lack of technical or managerial skills:* Organization believes that they either lack in content or context. In simple words, they lack the technical or managerial or interpersonal skills necessary for the success of the position. It could be because of the lack of aptitude,

14

exposure to certain opportunities or projects or lack of development opportunities or unwillingness to respond to the change in job requirements.

> *Lack of career skills:* These people are too engaged in their own island within the organization that they lose their usefulness across larger domains. These people lack the understanding of the big picture and are not considered fit for bigger roles.

> *Lack enough desire:* Some people let it be known explicitly that they do not seek promotion. This could be because of multiple reasons, such as personal, family or other reasons. If a person is seen to be having high potential, the organization may try and force development opportunities, eventually frustrating the individual.

For example, one of the leaders I have worked with said, '*When the organization was struggling with product quality, I built up the team for customer support and helped overcome challenges. For the past five years, our team grew, and I grew with it. Now the product quality issues have been fixed and the importance of my team has reduced. I have been so focused on support that I do not have any other skill. I am so stuck now in my career. I do not know what to do or where to start.*'

The paper presented that a person's career goes through a cycle of 'learning–maturing–promotion' before reaching the 'plateau'. And that there are three ways to exit the 'plateau'.

• *Obsolescence:* There is no further growth and over time the position loses the value. Lack of challenge, motivation or attention may lead to poor performance over time. Alternately, modernization or reorganization may make the function redundant. Or someone younger comes along with a better claim to the same position. This scenario results into a redundancy and the person eventually loses the job.

- *Terminal placement:* A promotion may result into a position which is beyond the capability of the individual. The performance dips below the expectations and despite performance improvement plans, the individual is not able to cope up. In such cases, the individual becomes redundant and loses the job. This is in line with 'Peter Principle', where an individual keeps on getting promoted till he/she reaches the level of incompetence.[2]

- *Successful plateauing:* The professional continues to evolve and develop with the support of the organization and remains a solid contributor on the plateau, forever.

There is another way to leave the plateau, but before we get there, let us have a look at the new business environment factors that may also lead to the plateau.

A DEPARTURE FROM OLD

There are many ways in which the modern organizations are different from the streamlined, vertical organizations of the old. Let us examine a few things that one must keep in mind when looking at career development in today's business world.

New Age Organizations

Newer organizations are relatively flatter. If there are not too many levels within the organization, quite a few of the employees will be reaching the peak potential positions and will stay on as key-contributors and remain highly valued. The plateauing is not really seen as the end of the career but a stage of development. Individual initiatives will determine the outcome of this type of plateauing. What you do during the time you are waiting for the promotion matters a lot, and it is not limited to just work.

Fast Growing Organizations

For a lot of start-ups and fast-growing organizations, there is a chance that younger and relatively less experienced people are leading the key positions. These people work hard and help the organization grow. As the organization grows, they need to stay relevant to the role or there are chances of external hires joining as their managers relegating these individuals to previous levels of contribution, creating an artificial plateau in their careers. Individuals need to be mindful of the organization's growth and the increasing demands of the role that they are undertaking. They have to continuously upskill and develop themselves to stay relevant to the organization and make sure they do not plateau.

Globalization

Globalization is not a new concept, but with technological advances, globalization has taken up a new pace, much faster than before. People who work in global organizations are overwhelmed with much more data, information and so on due to the increased connectivity. Leaders have to adopt a different mindset if they are to leverage the global opportunities and continue to help their organization grow. The inability to learn to leverage the globalization may lead you to plateau.

Where Is the Career Ladder?

There is no career ladder anymore. A decade or two back, when a person joined an organization, it was easy to figure out the ropes. You could see how various people have progressed and some became your role models. You seek opportunities to learn from them and in the process advance yourselves. The career was a natural progression.

Executives at mid and senior levels in multiple organizations agree that these days the organizations are in a constant flux. Every year, if not earlier, they change strategic directions. There are mergers, acquisitions, technological transformations, organizational transformations and so on. You may have a new manager every year. You lose all the history and credibility that you built by working hard and excelling over last year. Can you build from scratch again? Only to be reset at the end of the year!

Multiple Generations at Work

For the first time in history, we will have five generations at workplace, working hand in hand. But who owns the responsibility to make such multi-generational workplace happy and productive? If the leaders, that is the people in Stages 3 and 4 do not adapt to handle the difference and mould their styles, the workplace can be very stressful and challenging.

Leadership Is Now Different

Peter Drucker once said, '*While the leader of the past knew how to tell, the leader of the future will know how to ask.*'[3] This is an excellent viewpoint for today's leaders.

Members of a team, today, are not looking to their leaders to have all the answers. What they are looking for is a leader who is genuine and candid, who values the members of his or her team, respects their ideas and expertise, and is willing to listen to the suggestions before deciding on a new direction or course of action.

A leader needs to be ready to accept the presence of the team members who are smarter than him/her in a specific subject and should be able to lead a team full of smarter people.

Jack Welch (General Electric) mentioned in one of the interviews that the ability of a leader to successfully run large organizations in today's volatile, uncertain, complex and ambiguous (VUCA) world is based on just two words—trust and truth.[4] Your people should have enough trust on you to tell you the truth about the situation, so that you can take the right decisions at the right time, else by the time you will discover the truth, it will be too late.

Your team and your leadership must perceive you as a leader who has earned the right to lead. Only then do you stand a chance to the promotion that you seek.

HITTING THE PLATEAU

Despite all the changes in the business space, the plateau still exists and like we explored in the sections above, the plateau may have become broader than before. In smaller organizations such as a start-up, or highly matrixed organizations, many Stage 2 people may be experiencing the effects of plateau. Since only about 5 per cent of people reach Stage 4, majority of the Stage 3 people are likely to hit the plateau sooner or later, depending on the design of the organization. And as we discussed, this also depends on the speed at which the organization is growing. So, if one has crossed Stage 2 of the career contribution, he/she will almost inevitably encounter the plateau.

A manager once shared with me, '*I am in this position for last four years, my leader hints on some future possibilities but nothing seems to come out of these career discussions. I do not see the path forward. I feel so stuck.*' This is a clear sign that the manager had reached a plateau in his career.

EXITING THE PLATEAU WITH GROWTH

You read in the previous chapter that growth is linked with the contribution and there are many ways to increase your contribution to the organization. The idea behind this book is to provide you with the perspectives that you may have been missing or not giving enough importance to. If you want to exit the plateau with an elevation to the next stage, you need to do more. How can you be among the 5 per cent who reach Stage 4?

In the book *Hit Refresh*, by Satya Nadella, he says, '*Every person, organization, and even society reaches a point at which they owe it to themselves to hit refresh—to reenergize, renew, reframe, and rethink their purpose*'. His own career shows us the indirect path to the position of CEO. He has had diverse experiences successfully delivering on multiple roles.

Even if it is just 5 per cent that reach the next level, it still means that the possibility to move to Level 4 exists. Someone is going to get there, though the opportunities are few and far between. So, the main thing is to make sure that you have the best chances to grab the opportunity when it comes around. Make sure that you renew, rethink and re-energize yourself to be ready.

So, what other things there are? There are at least 10 things that you can do, and the fact is that each one of them is a tried and tested strategy. And these are apart from the domain competencies required to be successful at the role. Each of the 10 aspects has a chapter of their own and each chapter has a few things to enable you to understand, learn and apply the strategy:

- What does the strategy mean?

- The nature of the efforts involved in adopting the strategy.

- The expected results.

- Experience of a successful leader on that strategy.

- Questions to help you reflect and chart your own path.

You may choose one or more strategies to complement your efforts as you see fit. The leader's story shall help you to relate a particular strategy with your own situation and stage of development.

WHEN MUST ONE START WORKING ON THESE STRATEGIES?

It is never too late to start. And it is never too early as well. If you are in Stage 3 and are already experiencing plateau, well the time is now. You must choose a couple of strategies to start with, and then once they become a habit or start coming naturally, start with the next one. These strategies are like behaviours and it may not be easy to adopt them. That is where a context of stories from leaders and the reflective questions will help you understand and apply them.

If you are in Stage 2 and are looking to move into Stage 3, you can choose to work on a couple of these strategies and make them your strength even before you reach Stage 3. It will become far easier to navigate your path through Stage 3 and projecting yourself as an ideal choice for Stage 4.

If you are in Stage 1, this book may help you to understand quite a few aspects of promotion that seem mystical and hazy. This book may help you start understanding the aspects of work that are not related to your own personal efforts. It will also help you to understand that as you grow up, you need to be able to deal with much higher levels of uncertainty and ambiguity as compared to the time when you start the career. The stories from various leaders will help you to engage better with the organization. In short, if you are ready to invest some effort, others might soon start wondering at the effortless way in which your career will start progressing.

WHAT IS THERE IN STORE?

The 10 strategies are put together in no specific order, but some are more fundamental than the others.

1. We start with the importance of setting up the right goals. At every stage in your career, you make many decisions. Many times, you take decisions as they come and do not consider the long-term implications of individual decisions. Some decisions take you towards the plateau which will limit the scope of your growth.

2. Next, we discuss the issue of horizontal growth versus vertical growth. Growth is almost always assumed to be vertical, and comes with a bigger title, larger and diverse teams and of course more benefits. But how do you become ready for roles that require diverse experience?

3. This is followed by another fundamental aspect— 'relationships'. It surprises people when they learn that the quality of their work alone cannot guarantee their growth. Apart from your manager, you must have other sponsors willing to support you. Leaders must take personality differences in their stride and be able to forge common goals that bring people together.

4. In the next aspect we will cover the importance of right conversations. It is some key people who take decisions with regard to your next role. But how well do they know you? Do they trust you? They may know you through your work, but that just proves the subject matter expertise, which is just one part of the trust element. You also need to establish your character, especially your intent, which is done through the conversations that you have with these stakeholders.

5. Visibility and personal branding are very important to your growth. You may have great qualities and capabilities, but if the right stakeholders are unaware of you and your work, you may be at a disadvantage. What happens when work never gets attributed to you?

6. The world is not static, in fact it is VUCA. What you knew yesterday cannot keep you ahead tomorrow. The importance of continuous learning cannot be ignored, and when you ignore learning in the name of being too busy, you suffer in your own career.

7. A well-rounded individual is always preferred for top roles. Creating an impact beyond your boundaries may be a way to showcase your leadership capabilities beyond your current role. Such opportunities also help you to connect with the leadership teams beyond your own vertical and provide you with many chances to have great conversations.

8. You must be able to articulate what you need at the right forum, at the right time and in the right way. You may deserve it but if you do not ask for it, the decision-makers may wonder if you really want it. They may give the position away to someone who values that role more.

9. Diversity is a new way of life at work. Leaders must have the ability to leverage the diversity to the benefit of the organization. If you are not conscious of the value that diversity can add, you might create hurdles for your own growth.

10. Emotional intelligence (EI) helps the leader to connect with others at human level. It fosters empathy and understanding and helps a leader to forge strong bonds. It is one of the key strengths of a leader.

DO NOT WAIT

These strategies are designed to give you an insight into the 'not so clear' aspects of promotion. They answer the questions that have kept you wondering. You may start building the understanding on why some people get chosen over others and find answers to 'What more I should do to get the next promotion?' or 'How I can ensure that the organization gives me credit for my hard work and loyalty?' and so on.

Do not wait! Start with the next chapter that shares with you the most fundamental of the strategies, the one that everyone should know early in their career.

REFERENCES

1. Ference TP, Stoner JAF, Warren EK. Managing the career plateau. *Academy of Management Review.* 1977;2(4): 602–612.

2. Peter LJ. *Peter principle.* Available from: https://en.wikipedia.org/wiki/Peter_principle [Accessed 10 February 2020].

3. Goldsmith M. Is the role of a leader changing? *Harvard Business Review.* Available from: https://hbr.org/2007/11/is-the-role-of-a-leader-changi [Accessed 10 February 2020].

4. Roth D. *Jack Welch says only two words matter for leaders today: Truth and trust.* Available from: https://www.linkedin.com/pulse/truth-trust-crap-how-jack-welch-looks-leadership-today-daniel-roth/ [Accessed 10 February 2020].

3

GOAL SETTING

Remember those childhood moments when someone asked you,
'What do you want to do when you grow up?' As a child you
might have spun some nice story about how you wanted to be that
great doctor who changes the world. As a child your expectations
were limited just by your imagination and not the hard realities
of the world.

When you grew up, your world was shackled with the 'limited
possibilities', and you started looking at what is achievable from
your current position and started to just define the next milestones.
You became tuned to defining the next few milestones and not to
think beyond that. 'What is the point of looking too far?' You may
argue that no one can look that far into future.

Slow and steady progress to achieve that next milestone may
one day lead you to 'The Plateau', from where most paths lead
downhill. If you have reached 'The Plateau', you know better
already. One of the key reasons you may be stuck is the fact that
you may have left your imagination behind and just focused

on the near term. If you have not focused on a destination, you might as well have been wandering and not really making progress to realizing your potential.

You desire to find your place in the world. But the world is not a small place and the paths are limitless. So how do you know what path will lead to unleashing your potential?

GOAL IS DIFFERENT THAN THE PATH

Having a goal is more than having the next few milestones. When you are on a well-travelled career path, from your point of view, the next few milestones seem very clear—the next promotion and so on. You do not know where these milestones might eventually lead, but they sure look like progress. If you continue to progress on that path and reach a plateau, you may realize that the path you chose was not the best.

There may be many less-travelled paths which might lead to a great destination. But these small, off-roads usually scare you; you wonder if they are worth the risk and you just stay on the course and may reach that plateau anyway. If you had a goal in mind, you could have chosen a path that had the most chances to lead to it, rather than just achieve the next visible milestone.

Goal is like the guiding star. You continue to make progress by achieving new milestones, but you make sure that you are moving towards the guiding star. Every time you reach crossroads, you look at the guiding star and then choose your path. You do not let the better-looking path guide you to a new destination. Goal will help you plot the milestones and take less-travelled paths to achieve your true potential.

When you were a child and every year when they asked you the question, 'What do you want to do when you grow up?' you came up with a different answer. And each time the answer felt like more right than the last answer. You have the liberty to change your goals as and when you feel like. But not having the goals will make you just wander and get stuck at a plateau.

It is really important that you make some decisions about what you want to do over a slightly longer period of 5–10 years. I know that this may sound like that rhetorical interview question, 'What would you like to do in five years' time?' or 'Where do you see yourselves in five years?' Most of the time it may seem that such a question is irrelevant and unimportant. Why should you bother yourself with something so far away when you do not know much about what is going to happen in a year? My discussions with various leaders over time have led me to believe that having long-term goals has a significant impact on the career journey. Let us take a look at the career journey of two professionals.

MARY AND JASMINE

Mary does a great Job and is always appreciated by the manager. She does not have any specific role in mind, that she aspires to, but just wants to progress in the general sense of the word. Initially, Mary seems to make good progress. She continues to deepen her skills in the specific area that she has been working on and adds complementary skills as she picks up more responsibilities. Mary was a software programmer and when she gets promoted to become a team manager, she adds the skills for project management. As she progresses, she handles more and more complex tasks and does a great job every time. She continues to grow up to a become the leader for one particular function. Now the next role requires some understanding of diverse functions and Mary had never had the opportunity to work in those functions. Mary feels stuck despite making great progress all along.

Jasmine is clear that she wants to become one of the directors and seeks a coach early on. She is very curious about the skills and experiences required for the role and always looks for guidance from relevant people. Her coach helps her to build a road map to the role of the director. Jasmine starts along with Mary and works hard and gets her first promotion along with Mary. She then looks for a change and works in a different function, which is a part of the road map to get to the director's role. Since she starts afresh in the new role compared to other colleagues, Jasmine takes a little longer than Mary to get her next promotion. After this next promotion, she takes support from the organization to go on a sabbatical to pursue an MBA. She knows that an MBA is also one of the prerequisites for the role of the director. She comes back and picks up a lead role in a newly established vertical. Her track record and the MBA help in securing this critical role. By this time Mary has already taken up the function head role and seems very pleased with her progress. Within the next three years, Jasmine gains a lot of experience of running a business unit and has posted a great success. Jasmine has gained diverse experiences, completed an MBA and has successfully set-up a new function area for the organization. Jasmine gets promoted to the same level as Mary. Mary has been at that role for three years now and was expecting to grow, but her director is non-committal. A year later when the role for the director opens up, Jasmine gets chosen and Mary still does not have a path forward.

Mary is wondering what went wrong. She always did a great job, was appreciated for her contribution and made good progress as she went along.

Would you want to be Jasmine or Mary? The choice is yours. You can ignore the question about what you would like to do five years later, or you could take it seriously and drive your own career. You make decisions at various stages in the career and you always want to make the best decision. But the best decision in the short run may not be the best decision in the long run. A goal acts as a lighthouse, it helps you avoid the pitfalls and always points you to the right direction.

Now let us look at the story of a leader who excels at setting goals and living them every day.

****

RAVINDER DANG: THE GOAL IS NOT WORTH CHASING IF THE JOURNEY IS NOT FUN

He brings a burning passion to photography, as he does to running. It is the same sense of deep commitment and passion that Ravinder Dang takes to his job. As Vice President Commercial Excellence of Asia Pacific and the General Manager of Baxter India, Ravinder has been leading the organization since 2016.

Ravinder believes that his journey that spans 27 years with experience across different industries opened his mind and widened his horizons. He was clear about his goals from the beginning, '*Unless you focus on your goals almost on a daily basis, you may not be serious about achieving them.*' says Ravinder. He believes that one must discover one's core values and strengths and align it to the career goals. It is impossible to fake passion, and without passion the outcomes will be mediocre. Add to it, consistency and perseverance and you are on the path to success.

Let us learn from his professional and personal journey so far.

The Professional Journey: Spanning Industries and Roles

After graduating in Life Sciences from the University of Delhi, he completed his MBA from Institute of Management Technology, Ghaziabad in 1993. Campus recruitment took him to Max India Ltd as a management trainee in pharmaceutical business learning sales, supply chain and marketing. Though his initial bias was to get more marketing experience as it was considered 'hot', Ravinder chose to move to sales and joined CIBA Vision, a division of Novartis India Ltd. From area manager, he quickly rose to become a regional manager and later moved into product management. His hunger for learning pushed him to seek more responsibility and he demonstrated high commitment to various roles he undertook. As he continued to perform, his scope of work increased dramatically.

After spending seven years in healthcare, Ravinder decided to change Industries. In 2000, he joined Anand Bazar Patrika's leading business magazine, *Businessworld*, as product manager. Skills and understanding of management principles have universal application across industries. His move from pharmaceuticals to media was seamless and he moved on to become circulation head and subsequently chief marketing officer. During his tenure at *Businessworld*, its direct marketing campaign won the Golden Lion at Cannes, France. Ravinder recalls, *'Getting my hands on the Cannes Lion was a high point of my tenure at Businessworld.'* The magazine at that time was breaking new grounds and became the highest circulating business magazine in India. *'Every week talking to my journalist colleagues as they shaped stories around the theme of the new economy left a lasting impression on me and was a wonderful learning experience'* says Ravinder.

In 2004, Ravinder came across an interesting opportunity of leading a business vertical at India's largest paper company. Ballarpur Industries Limited (BILT) had forayed into consumer products and had aggressive plans for the business. Seeing the scope of the role and the possibility of shaping a new business, Ravinder accepted the role of Head, Retail Business at BILT. The consumer was evolving and seeking differentiated products. For driving rapid growth, it was critical that the business be at the cutting edge of innovation. His team aggressively developed new line extensions of their three flagship brands BILT Matrix, Ten on Ten student notebooks and the premium Royal Executive Bond paper. They focused on building the distribution channel and used innovative marketing approaches to grow the business.

Tasting success in this line, the board of BILT supported the launch of the Office Supplies Retail vertical. This demanded new processes, competencies and adaptability. The team launched pilot stores across Delhi, Mumbai, Pune and Bangalore, and established an online B2B vertical serving large corporates across India. The business under Ravinder's leadership grew from ₹13 Cr to nearly ₹300 Cr over six years. He proved once again that his skills could span industries and that he could create success with different teams.

He then moved to Metro Cash & Carry in Bangalore and led the SCO vertical (Institutions) Unit. This was a short stint, but it exposed him to the principles of disaggregating businesses into key consumption levers.

In 2012, Ravinder moved back to Gurugram and joined Baxter as Business Unit Director, medication delivery. He became the India Business Leader in 2016 and shaped a strong turnaround of the business. Today he leads India business as well as the commercial excellence function for Asia Pacific. Further Ravinder is the leader of the Med Tech Forum at NATHEALTH, a multi-stakeholder industry body and also is part of the National Executive Board at AMCHAM.

Baxter has been a big learning journey; his experience includes working in a multicultural environment, shaping team performances to deliver consistently on organization goals, promoting inclusion and diversity, apart from excelling in business.

Over the years, all his career transitions were driven by a strong desire to seek greater challenges. Those challenges facilitated continuous learning and grew him as a professional. He engages with his job deeply, keeps an eye on his personal and professional goals and constantly looks to contribute in a bigger way.

Long-Term Goals Should Link to Your Short-Term Development

As a student of business management, Ravinder was ambitious. He has used every opportunity to learn and prepare himself for the role ahead. '*I have always been quite ambitious. I wanted to achieve a certain level of professional and leadership competence and I was willing to go the extra mile for it.*'

While reflecting on his journey Ravinder laments that in his initial years, he did not seek mentoring and coaching. While he was clear about the long-term goals, he did not ask questions such as 'What are the opportunities of immediate improvement?' 'Where do you think I can deliver better?' 'What should we do in the next six months?' and so on to create short-term growth plan. He says '*Probably, I felt a little insecure but with time it has become much easier. Now, the regular development conversations help me with my focus and possibilities of improvement in everyday work.*'

Principles of Individual Growth

Ravinder's career stands on bedrock of three principles.

He has a '(6 + 12) month window' rule. He gives himself this time to make a difference in any role. Six months to shape the agenda and twelve months to deliver on that goal. He works in 90-day sprints, this allows him to focus strongly on the current goal while he seeks feedback from his colleagues and his supervisor to ensure that he is not missing the 'woods for the trees'.

One of the principles of career growth which he has intuitively followed is diversity of the roles. He says, '*I have done a variety of roles including sales, marketing and leading key projects. I have worked in different industries, contexts and applied my skills and gained new ones through those experiences. I like to work hard and engage deeply to make a meaningful difference.'*

He remembers from his days at Business world that he was the only marketing professional who used to show up for edit meetings. He used to deep dive into discussions, share his perspectives as a circulation head and had many great conversations with journalists. Some of these conversations have stayed with him forever. A recent similar experience has been the Function Excellence project he has led at Baxter in APAC. It gave him the opportunity to gain insights on how functions operate and what are the possibilities of engaging with them to deliver strong business outcomes.

The second principle is always to seek challenges. He says, *'If it is not challenging then there is no fun in chasing it.'* Even in his current role, he has been seeking projects that can help his organization to drive growth and innovation. He has been fortunate to get the opportunity to lead many such projects and has gained from those experiences.

The third principle is that *'You do not need to be perfect to succeed, 70 per cent is good enough'*. Since his days as a student, he was committed to be a successful professional. But there were parts of the journey when he had doubts and thought, *'Maybe, I do not have it in me, Maybe I missed a trick and do not have the X-Factor.'* It could be tough faith-shaking moments when you get feedback that you do not have a certain quality or a specific skill and so on needed for your goal. Ravinder believes that a lot of people lose their path and vision at that point in time. That is when you need to tell yourself that you do not need to be perfect. Imperfection does not mean you will not win one day; it only means that like everyone else you have room for improvement. Consider the feedback constructively and keep imbibing new stuff to keep growing.

Connect to Your Core

His mantra is stay deeply connected to your core—your purpose, values and your strengths.

Ravinder says that he was an average student in school. He says, *'When I got out of the management college, I thought at that time that the only way I could create a place for myself, is by achieving some level of professional and leadership competence. If I did not achieve it, I would be a "nobody" and that would be a bitter pill to swallow.'*

As Ravinder continued on his professional journey he realized that professionalism, self-awareness, learning agility and hard work were his enablers. He is demanding and constantly measures himself against these values. Sharing more about hard work he says, *'A British quote which motivates me is that "no one died of hard work." So, if it is required for me to put in 15–16 hours of working on a day to get a job done, I would do just that.'* So, if it was a tough day, or a tough week or a tough month, he would just square-up his shoulders and get on with his work.

He often links a tough patch to running a hard marathon and tells himself 'one mile at a time'. He says, *'It boils down to knowing what you want, reflecting deeply on what you bring to the game, engage with passion and play to win.'*

Building Blocks

Ravinder believes that you set out to achieve a few things in life and you chase them down with all your heart. Never give up on those dreams. It may take longer than you planned and that is probably because one does not fully understand the lay of the land or what it takes to achieve that goal, but if it is important to you then you will keep at it. It is non-negotiable.

While executing your goals, your main focus should be directed to shaping behaviours that will help you achieve the goal. So, let us say you want to improve your communication skills and you decide to develop behaviours related to listening to start with. Then you must concentrate on your behaviour—take feedback, work on that change. As long as you are making progress you are moving along.

Second, you must make sure that you have adequate preparedness for the goal. Figure out the resources, ask for help wherever you need. You need to get into battle with odds in your favour.

Review and Reflect

Ravinder believes that long-term goals are achievable only if one reviews progress regularly. He uses technology and apps that track his habits and goals. Both for his workouts and daily reading objectives. He breaks big goals into small achievable targets. Small milestones are achievable and, consistent and steady progress make you reach your goal.

Ravinder believes that there could be instances of conflict in situations, but if you are really connected with your core purpose and values, you will know the right thing to do. He says at times he has to choose between his hobbies like running in the morning versus a work commitment. Similarly, as a leader he also ensures his teams have enough flexibility to support a healthy mix of personal and professional targets.

He believes that he will always be 'work in progress'. Extremely demanding from himself, he has come across many good leaders in his career who have been both good coaches and mentors. He has learnt to actively seek feedback and has worked on it. He acknowledges support at home as well. Ravinder says, *'My wife, Priya is my coach and critic. She is herself a successful professional in her own right and constantly lets me know where I stand. I think it is powerful to have someone who can help you on your journey of growth and progress.'*

Many Bricks Build a Wall

In 2012, he discovered through a photography workshop that he has strong visual acumen. Over time, Ravinder has visited interesting places for his shoots and dabbled in multiple streams of photography, including wildlife, street and landscape. He partnered with a friend who published a book on spiritualism *Joyful Living* which carries pictures shot by him to convey the stories in the book.

Towards the end of 2013, Ravinder started working on his health goals. He jokes about it and says, '*The foodie in me has been fond of eating and I had been eating without care for a while. One day I stepped on the scale and it read 110 kilos.*' He decided that it was time to work on his health. He took to running. '*It all started with a fun 5K, which led to a local 10K race.*' Then one day a friend pushed him for a half marathon in 2015 and he remembers finishing it with cramps. Always a sucker for challenges, finishing with cramps was just the trigger he needed for bigger goals in running. Now he runs full marathons and is chasing his dream to run all the six world majors. He competed in Berlin in 2019 and this year plans to run London and Chicago marathon.

Both these hobbies complete him and add balance to his life.

Photography helps in his creative expressions and running gives him focus and helps him to stay physically fit. He says, '*Now I understand how fitness helps me perform better at work.*'

What Can Organizations Do to Encourage Goal Setting?

Ravinder believes that organizations tend to be complex and he advises leaders to work very hard on simplifying things. Also, he believes that leadership should ensure authenticity around core values. Conversations on core values have to be instilled deeply in actions, otherwise they lose their meaning. That is what aligns people, allows them to set their goals that make their work meaningful. That is how organizations become sustainable ecosystems where individuals and teams thrive.

How Does He Mentor His Team on Goals?

Ravinder talks to his direct reports every month, where they focus on the goals and discuss what is working and what is not. He focuses on how he can help them. They have deep conversations around learning and development.

As a team they celebrate culture and values every month. At Baxter they have four core values: Speed, Courage, Simplicity and Collaboration. Whenever anyone demonstrates any of these values, they celebrate. This promotes the right culture. He creates opportunities for people to contribute and learn by participating in cross-functional projects. These are voluntary assignments and one must raise their hand to get engaged as these require extra effort. He encourages deep engagement and learning by doing through diverse experiences.

What Ravinder Says about Your Next Promotion

Ravinder says that if you are at a mid-level management role, there is a long way to go. '*We all imagine a plateau and start throwing that word around casually.*' Most of the times it is a mental construct or a perception. If you feel stuck, it is time for you to have a conversation with right people or seek mentoring.

He offers the following suggestions:

First have an aggressive goal that is aligned to your core values. If you do what you love and love what you do, you set out to make a difference in the world, you will be recognized. Success will definitely come your way.

Second, focus on behaviours which are consistent with your future direction. For example, if you want to be a strong business leader, identify the specific competencies which you need to build and set out to build

> **Message for Millennials**
>
> Ravinder's advice to the millennials is to be conscious about their work ethic and professionalism. Leaders tend to offer more opportunities to the professionals with the strongest work ethic, so try to have one.

those competencies one step at a time. Feel free to have a conversation with your manager or your peers and seek feedback on what you need to change and then start working on it.

Third, he believes in diversity of experiences, the importance of a challenging task and the power of unconscious learning. He says that if you do your everyday job with a lot of commitment and a lot of engagement, then the unconscious learning is deep.

Next, he says, even if a job seems mundane you must do it with high level of professionalism. Core values such as hard work and authenticity give you the velocity towards your goal. You may not count on yourself for being the smartest in the team, but you must count on yourself for the values and for the spirit you bring to the game as a leader or a team player.

Ravinder says that you must focus on your goal and stay on course. A journey of thousand miles is completed a step at a time. You must focus on developing yourself and delivering your best, always.

****

WHAT STOPS YOU FROM SETTING THE GOALS

Your routine tasks, your business or your fears can come in your way when you want to work on your goals. You may even be hampered by the effort it takes to get them right or may not be motivated enough to take up the task. Sometimes, lack of examples or role models may also hold you back as it is easy to emulate but not so easy to be a pioneer. The brief pointers below may help you identify what factors are holding you back, if at all.

Life Goes On

Career is not the only thing in your life, and you are usually busy doing one thing or the other. Even in office, business as usual takes priority, and you are busy handling routine issues. You do not have a timeslot carved out for career planning. Career is something that happens when you try doing your best at work. Mostly, your goals are set by your organization and you may believe that the easiest path to a great career is to try and surpass those. You do not get much time to think and plan your own career goals.

Quantifying Desires Is Tough

It is a difficult task. It is easy to dream and desire a designation, a salary. But, sitting down and working on the clarity needs focus, time and patience. Sometimes you may have questions and if you

In a Harvard study conducted years back, researchers found that only 13 per cent of the graduates from its 1979 MBA program had goals. Just 3 per cent of them had their goals clearly written down and had created plans to accomplish them.

Ten years later, they found out that the 13 per cent who had goals were earning twice compared to those who had no goals. And the 3 per cent who wrote down their goals were earning 10 times!![1]

do not know where to find the answers or do not have anyone who can answer those questions, doubts creep in and you are not able to conclude. Sometimes you may get contradictory advice and are not able to agree on the final expectations because of the confusion. And, sometimes in this information overload world, there are endless paths to choose from and you do not want to commit.

Fears Can Hold You Back

What if I chose wrong goals? What if things change and my goals become useless? What if I set goals too high? What will I have to do if I set the goals? What if I do not have the ability to achieve my goals? What if I fail? Fear can hold you in the comfort zone and you may like to sit and think about the goals and even discuss them with others but not actually set them up.

Complacency Creates Stagnation

Goal setting requires great effort. If you are a little lazy, you may postpone this hard work to later, let us say next week. And this will happen to you a few times. Then things may change a bit and new considerations may emerge, requiring you to gather more information. You delay gathering this information and by the time you are ready, things may have changed again.

Not Motivated Enough

I am making good progress. What more can I expect? I am earning more than my friends from college; I must be doing well. Why bother setting goals when I am making steady progress? You do not know your potential but are happy with what you have achieved and so you are not really motivated to stretch yourself.

Make It Happen

I hope that by now you believe that this is one of the most important activity as part of the career planning and are ready to take steps. I do hope that you have identified the factors that hold you back. Ravinder's story provided above must have given you the required motivation to get started on the task of defining goals. The section below highlights the pitfalls you must avoid when working on your goals.

Cut the Fluff

First, setting goals is not a formality, it is not 'tick in the box' or another task on the list. Even if you are setting the goals on the request of your organization as part of the development planning, please own it completely and do it for yourself. Do not feel like it is a fad and that nobody really cares. You should care and that is all that matters.

1. *Be precise and clear:* Identify the roles that you would want to do, not the titles that you want to have for example:

   a. National Head of Sales for the Banking Vertical (of an IT organization) is more precise than VP Sales for a large IT organization.

   b. Handling 200 Mn $ in annual sales is more precise than leading a team of 20 salespeople.

2. *Not glamorized:* Make sure the goals are very realistic. For example:

   a. To be a great leader.... is not a goal.

   b. To turn around the organization... is a bit too lofty and does not define your role in it.

   c. Leading the sales for a country... is more realistic.

41

Be Ready

Goals are like defining your own strategy, and it may mean saying 'No' to certain opportunities. There may be sacrifices or pains associated. Are you ready for that? Are you ok to go through the path and accept the trade-offs for the chance to bring to life the exciting outcome you have planned? For example:

1. You want to lead the research and development (R&D) for one set of products globally, and you are making great achievements and adding new patents. Your manager offers you a promotion to lead a new vertical, but this will take you away from the product line that you so love. You can get the promotion in your chosen path but that will take up a few years longer. Would you be willing to let that promotion go and take your chances?

2. You want to excel in product marketing and grow to be the leader for the online media for the global organization. There is an opportunity to lead sales for a region with a promotion; would you let it go in favour of an assignment at your current level that gives you an opportunity to start learning the online media marketing?

3. Would you be willing to relocate without your family to get a two-year international business experience that will be essential for the role that you seek?

Set Your Priorities

Conflicting priorities are painful. If you have too many goals and they are conflicting, nothing good will come out of them. Most of us want to grow in the careers and live happy lives and engage with the society at large. But everything may not be achievable at the same time. So, it is good to set the priorities right. Do not set competing goals, it may be wiser to space things out.

Stay Focused

Goals certainly provide the clarity. But you need not be obsessed with them; instead of focusing on goals all the time, you must focus on how to achieve them in your world. I mean you must not be reviewing your goals every now and then. Goals are longer term and it takes time before you can review progress and decide any changes.

1. *Be consistent:* Act every day or every week as per your plan.

2. *Be accountable:* You must own the goals and drive the actions. Review progress against the goals every quarter and correct course when needed.

3. *Review goals:* Once a year you need to see if these goals are still what you want. If you have achieved some parts, you must then set new targets.

When in Doubt?

Whenever you have choices, you must reflect on your goals and see where you want to go. It will help anchor your path on the right direction and help you make the right choice. It will need courage to say 'No' to good options and stay true to the plans.

TRANSFORM YOUR MINDSET

The growth mindset will help you set the right goals and effectively chart the path too.

FIXED MINDSET	GROWTH MINDSET
I do not have time for goal setting.	How can I find time to set my goals?
Nobody understands what I want to do?	Who can help me to set my goals better?

FIXED MINDSET	GROWTH MINDSET
I do not need to change my goals.	Goals need to be reviewed periodically.
I am afraid that goals may bind me.	Goals provide a direction for my efforts and I have the flexibility to adjust them.
Not every goal can be achieved.	I need to set achievable goals and continue to add new goals as I achieve some.

GOAL SETTING: IN ACTION

Reflecting on the following few questions will help you in identifying your goals and some of the milestones on that path.

- What is it that you would like to achieve professionally in the next five years?

- What is it that you would like to achieve professionally in the next one year?

- How motivating is your goal to you?

- How comfortable are you with the goal?

- How do you feel while thinking about the moment when you will achieve it?

- What pain areas do you see associated with the goal? For example, timings, travel, doing some boring work and so on.

- How ready are you for the associated pains? And what are you going to do about it?

- How committed do you feel to this goal?

- How achievable is it for you?

- How is it going to make your life better?

- Which of your strengths could help you to achieve the goal?

- What else needs to happen for achieving this goal?

- What are the habits you need to develop to achieve this goal?

- What can you do about it today, this month and quarter?

The habit of acting every day on one or more of your major goals is life-transforming.

Brian Tracy

REFERENCE

1. Integrated Wealth Systems. *What Harvard's goal setting survey results reveal.* Available from: https://integratedwealthsystems.com/harvard-results-on-goal-setting/ [Accessed 10th February 2020].

4

HORIZONTAL GROWTH

❝ ❞
Your greatness is measured by your horizons.
MICHELANGELO

Google is one of the most sought-after employers. But it is not a 'run of the mill' organization. I say that for multiple reasons but the reasons that are most relevant to us are career growth and organizational structure. Google employs a relatively flat organization structure. Google is not the only one, there are many others who are built on a similar approach. Most of the work happens in cross-functional teams. An individual could be on multiple teams at any given point and contribute based on his/her role on the team. If you are working for such an organization, will there be a single leader who will be evaluating your performance and helping you on your career journey? The answer is a simple 'No'. In fact, the way your performance is measured is also an involved process. So how do you grow?

Also, irrespective of the organization structure, as you reach the mid-level management, there comes a point in your career where you need a much broader perspective to achieve that next promotion.

PROMOTION IN A NEW AGE ORGANIZATION

What does promotion mean in a flatter organization? If you are an individual contributor and the next promotion does not expand your scope of work, but gives you a bigger title and more salary, will you consider it a promotion? You may enjoy working from project to project for some time, working on just one aspect, and you may get to support bigger projects as you grow and maybe more complex ones; but then what? You may then try some other aspects of projects and diversify your experience; but will that lead you to the top management?

Flatter structures are difficult to navigate and because of a lean middle management, there is a big gap between one role and the next. Many flatter organizations hire externally because of the lack of well-rounded talent within the organization. And many people leave the flatter organizations in order to get the growth they want, and there are many such examples on Glassdoor.[1] But what if you join another flat organization with a bigger title and more salary and your problem remains?

THE PROBLEM OF BIG GAP

The flat organization structure is just one specific case where the vertical growth is not always the right way. This phenomenon is also seen at the level of mid management in most of the organizations where beyond a particular stage the professionals find themselves 'plateaued'. Consider the following case:

An executive in a software services organization leads the development vertical for retail segment and has the aspirations to become the CIO. He reports into the overall development head who takes care of the retail, B2B and emerging business segments. He has two peers, one who leads the B2B and the other who leads the emerging business. Each a specialist, in their own right, having built the skills and capabilities through years of experience leading projects and teams across the country.

The development head in turn reports in to the CIO who leads other functions such as operations, quality, deployment and so on in addition to the development. Each of which has their own heads who are the peers for the development head. Refer to the picture here.

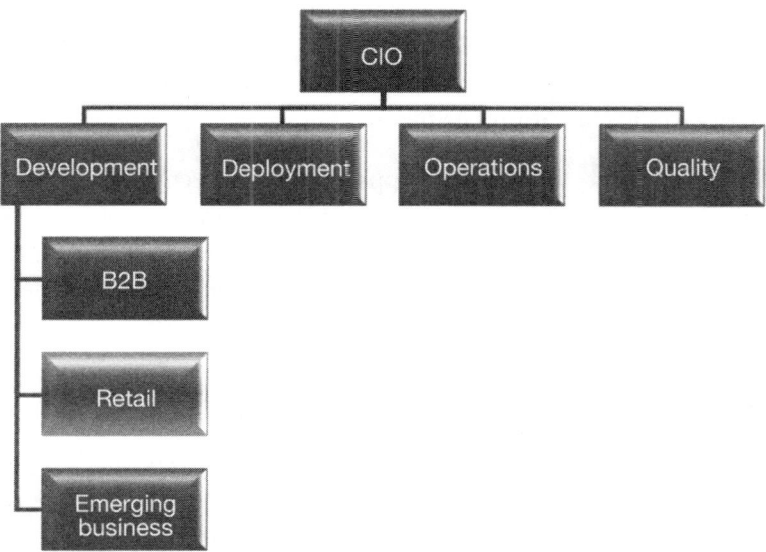

This executive does not have a clear path to the CIO role. Do you agree? What experiences would one look for, if one were to look for a CIO? Do you think doing his own role for a few more years can make the executive ready for the development head role? What would be the best course of action for this person?

What about the development head? Can he/she claim the CIO role easily? What experiences are required for the CIO role? Is the gap between the roles of development head and CIO also big?

At the top of the organization where various functions merge, the requirement is of the people who can claim the understanding of various functions and not just one. But if you always focus on vertical growth, you may find yourself into a very specific predicament. Similar scenario exists in global organizations where a country leader may aspire to lead a region but may lack suitable experiences and abilities to claim the role. Scenarios like this are very common at the very top of the organization. Many executives get stuck at this level and never find their way out. Just like flat organizations, many people leave jobs to seek career growth and some just settle for same role in a bigger organization and do find themselves in similar predicament.

Evolved organizations offer support to the executives through multiple ways. They create succession plans and create a long-term program for grooming certain individuals who are chosen as potential successors and ensure a smooth transition to new roles. But even they can support just a few people.

YOUR GROWTH IS YOUR RESPONSIBILITY

Many professionals get plateaued as they struggle to navigate their careers. The organizations may not always be able to support individuals for their growth so the onus for growth falls back to you. What can you do to change your situation and when is the right time to start thinking about it?

We talked about goal setting in the previous chapter, and also compared the career paths of Mary and Jasmine. Did you notice how deliberately Jasmine chose to take horizontal movements multiple times in the career, and though in the short run it cost her extra years to reach the same position, and in the long run Jasmine was able to reach the goal that she set in the beginning. Did you also notice that Jasmine took charge of the career from the very beginning and continued the efforts all along? She must have put in extra effort in learning new things every time she took a jump sideways.

When do you think it is right to make such sideways moves, early in career or later in career? There is no right or wrong time to make these moves, it depends on your awareness and opportunities. Gathering more experiences early in your career will surely be helpful.

Given the cases, we discussed earlier and the tendencies of businesses adopting more flatter approaches, it is imperative that you will come across a career plateau, where the next role that you are looking at, seems like a very big jump in terms of capability. It is prudent to acknowledge your situation, tighten your belt and set on to the path of 'horizontal growth'. The horizontal growth may not give you immediate rewards and you will have to put in a lot more effort to maintain the success that you have achieved so far in your vertical growth, but this will reduce the gap between you and the role you aspire. After successful horizontal role(s), you will be ready for the vertical growth that you have been eyeing from the beginning. Never let your target role out of your sight, it will help you plan the right moves to improve your stature and eligibility for it.

Let us now look at the story a leader who has benefitted from the horizontal growth multiple times in his career and has reached the position that he aspired to.

****

ARINDAM HALDAR: BRAND EXPERT'S JOURNEY TO THE CEO'S ROLE

Arindam loves challenges! They keep him charged and going. After his graduation from IIT Kharagpur and post-graduation from IIM Calcutta, he got his first job at Colgate-Palmolive. It was a dream job for many and came with a promise of great potential, but it was not enough for him. He left that career path to pick up something more challenging. He took up different roles by making horizontal moves, broadening his scope and gaining much needed experience. His ability to challenge himself by going outside his comfort zone and taking up a bigger mantle led him to his current role as the CEO of a leading diagnostics organizations. The path was not easy, and neither was it straight, each step came with its own challenges and learnings. He says, '*Where is the fun in a straight and easy path?*'

He also claims barring some exceptions, careers do not tend to have relatively straight path. He says, '*It is not your performance but potential that moves you up. You take a criss-cross path to the top and the ladder that finally takes you to the top role may not be the one you started climbing when you began your journey.*'

A Great Beginning: The First Horizontal Move

Arindam joined Colgate-Palmolive as a Management Trainee, fresh out of IIM Calcutta campus in 1995. His first profile was as an intern in sales and marketing. It involved a 13-month rotational training program with various assignments in field sales and brand marketing along with exposure to other departments. On completing his internship, he was assigned as a Sales Manager in Kolkata, his hometown.

Typically, newly inducted management graduates spend about three years in the field before they are inducted in marketing and brand management, but Arindam was offered a role in brand management within a year of sales experience after the management trainee stint; an indication of recognition of his performance and calibre. He moved as Product Manager, Colgate Dental cream; the flagship brand of Colgate; in Mumbai, the headquarters of Colgate. Brand marketing was a great opportunity for Arindam to learn and was a strategic role with immense potential. Even though this was not a promotion and primarily a horizontal move, Arindam was happy that he had achieved what he had sought.

A Small Cog in a Big Machine

Despite being a part of the flagship brand of the country, after sometime, Arindam started feeling dissatisfied, though at that time, he did not know what the problem was. He was doing quite well for himself, but something just did not feel right. After a lot of introspection, it was clear to him that this was not what he wanted to do and despite opposition from family and friends, he resigned without a fallback job, having worked with Colgate for three years.

With the hindsight of experience, Arindam talks about his decision to leave Colgate.

'I really wanted to make a difference but as Colgate was the flagship brand, my contribution in decision making, creativity and freedom to take initiative was very limited and I started feeling boxed in. One needs to have the ability to step back and see things in perspective. But back then, I did not have the wisdom that comes with experience and I just took the decision solely basis my "inner voice."'

To the Smaller Pond!

Fortunately, Arindam got his next opportunity to work for Godrej Pillsbury in Bangalore in the year 1998. Though Pillsbury was a big brand in the USA, it was hardly known in India at that time. He joined as area sales manager and became a part of the launch team of 'Pillsbury Chakki Fresh Atta' in Bangalore.

'Even though people around me thought of it as a retrograde move, I felt that it was a pleasant change. The contrast was remarkable—from a small fish in a big pond to a relatively mid-sized fish in a much smaller pond!! I was very excited to be a part of the process of launching a multi-billion-dollar global brand in India, though at that time I was not sure how long I would stay at Pillsbury. I however enjoyed the challenge of launching a new product and I still take pride in sharing that I sold the first pack of Pillsbury Atta (Flour) in the country on 13 March 1998.'

53

The first six years of Arindam's career are typical of a premier B-School pass out; from management trainee to sales and then to brand management, but with one key difference—the change from Colgate to Pillsbury. This reflects not only his willingness to accept change and new challenges but also speaks volume about his inner desire to make a difference. Had he not taken the decision of moving out of a perceived good role in a great company and seek a horizontal move, he would have been deprived of great experiences that came with the change.

Pillsbury was subsequently acquired globally by General Mills in 2001 and Arindam became a part of the new organization. In the new organization, he got many interesting opportunities. Every time he had the inkling of boredom setting in, he was pushed out of his comfort zone into the deeper side of the pool into a new role and opportunity. He stayed in General Mills for about 17 years and worked in 7 different roles.

The First Big Departure: A Risk Worth Taken

His first big departure from the story book career happened in 2001 when he was given the opportunity to start the export business of General Mills, a Profit and Loss (P&L) responsibility. This role was offered to him by his mentor, who believed Arindam would be suitable for setting up business from scratch. He had great faith and confidence in his abilities to make the new business a success.

'It was an exciting opportunity for me. It was a start-up within a start-up and gave me a lot of freedom to paint the white canvas with my own colours'.

However soon after he joined the new profile, his manager and mentor left the organization, and he started reporting directly to the India Managing Director. This was a huge responsibility as well as a great opportunity.

'I took a risk in picking up this role, and my career was at stake. The business was risky to start with, as everything had to be built grounds up. However, I took advantage of the fact that it was early in my career and I had the appetite to take big risks.'

The genesis of the business was the unfulfilled need for 'taste of home' in food amongst Indians settled overseas, and their willingness and ability to pay for the right quality. He says, *'I started with a market research including meeting potential customers—Indians settled abroad in UK, USA and other countries. The role involved extensive travel; I was young and there was such a charm in this opportunity; visiting so many countries for the first time with a suitcase in hand and setting up things from scratch, getting the feel of an entrepreneur. We made innovations in the entire range of Indian flat breads, including ready to puff rotis, authentic* adraki aloo *paratha (ginger potato flat bread) and stuffed naans, to suit the needs of the target market. It gave me great satisfaction to get the opportunity to connect the Indian diaspora to their roots through food. The business started clocking revenue in more than a hundred crores and was the first profitable business for the India unit.'*

Arindam also got an opportunity to be a part of the team that set up the factory for these frozen products in India. These diverse experiences gave him an entrepreneurial experience and an opportunity to prove his worth in the company. The role came with incredible operating freedom in managing the business division.

'I got an opportunity to present my business to the Global Leadership teams along with other business leaders. I was applauded for creating a new business, making it big and profitable. I started enjoying my freedom and success and was thinking how great I was doing, and that the next role should be even bigger. But I was in for a shock! I was hand-picked for a new role about which initially I felt devastated.'

The Hard Push: A Boon in Disguise

Another horizontal move was awaiting him, one that would take him away from the freedom of the entrepreneur role he so cherished, but would become the launch pad for the next stage in his career. However, to understand this aspect of Arindam's challenge, it is important to go back and look at the surrounding environment.

As shared earlier, General Mills bought Pillsbury in 2001. These two companies, very old competitors in the USA (over a 100 years), had grown in size very differently and had different processes and cultures. The top management of the two companies understood the challenges of integrating the two very culturally diverse and financially equal companies (both having more than USD 5 Billion turnover) built over a long time. Hence, they did not go headlong into integration and took a slower and more measured path. The US-based offices of the two companies took up to four years to merge and integrate.

'The coming together of these two organizations was like a marriage of two equals and the merger and integration required a lot of effort and strategy. It would not be wrong to say that both the companies did this part very well.'

After they were through with the US integration, they focused their attention on their international units. India was chosen to be one of the five pilot countries globally for the integration process. The company went about this phase of integration in the same cautious but effective manner and enrolled local staff to lead the business transformation. Arindam was hand-picked by the India MD and was given the role of leading this significant business transformation. He was initially not inclined to take up the challenge and hated his leader and circumstances for the same, but after his supervisor explained the importance of the task at hand and based on feedback from his other mentors, he took up the challenge, though he was still sceptical. After a few years, Arindam thanked his leader for pushing him into the role. He acknowledges that he is lucky to have had such a farsighted manager in his life.

'*The first few months were very frustrating as I had gotten so used to my independence in the earlier profile. It was a humongous task to rewrite business processes right from sales forecasting, demand planning to running Rough Cut Capacity Planning, Material Requirement Planning, vendor scheduling, long-range business planning with one set of numbers running across the company. I had to work with people who were senior to me not only in age but experience as well, and I was telling them to do things differently from what they had being doing of the last 20–30 years. It was not easy. The major learning from this role was how to influence people over whom you do not have any direct authority. The project got the nomenclature of Process Excellence and Knowledge (PEAK). I saw early success first with the factories which transformed within a year followed by the business units which progressively moved to new processes and we got good adoption within two years.*'

The Project Leadership Team of PEAK got recognized with the Global Champions Award in 2009—the highest honour at General Mills Inc. Arindam still has the plaque in his office and sounded very happy and excited while showing the 'Champions Award Memento'.

He acknowledges that once he successfully completed the Business transformation role, all other future roles became easier for him.

Fast-Paced Growth: Building On

After posting a big success in the transformation role, Arindam got another boost in his career and in 2008, he was selected in an operational role as Director, Häagen-Dazs, a part of General Mills. He not only introduced the business in India but also took another challenge of establishing a new type of food business based on food service retail operation and consumer facing brand outlets.

'*This was new to the Indian operation and I spent time learning about this business in Singapore. To understand every minute detail of the business,*'

I actually worked in Häagen-Dazs ice cream lounges in Singapore, scooping ice cream for customers along with doing odd jobs in the store. I wanted to feel the job in its natural environment before working on building the business in India.'

Needless to say, Arindam was successful and he was rewarded with another growth. He became Director of Premium Foods Business Unit in 2010. Additionally, he was made a member of the Global Marketing Council.

An Adventure of a Different Sort

Even as he was doing great at General Mills, the India unit remained relatively small. He was looking to join a bigger company in a larger role to be able to make a much more significant impact. To fulfil his quest, he left the 'comfort zone' of working with large global companies and joined Sterlite Technologies, an India-based MNC. Sterlite, a telecom manufacturing and infrastructure company, had huge growth plans in the home broadband segment and was looking for a P&L head to set up their retail business. However, before taking up the role in retail business, Arindam was asked to help Sterlite Tech to establish their brand and create shareholder value.

'The next couple of years at Sterlite were probably some of the most challenging and testing. I was learning about the products, solutions and teaching teams about brand building. Brand is like a halo, and it is largely invisible but makes one distinctive and special. The role gave me an opportunity to apply my skills to an alternate industry and prove my worth once again. But while I was working to build the brand, I was also looking to get back to main-stream operations role.'

Zooming to CEO Role!

Arindam's next move was to become the chief operating officer (COO) of SRL Diagnostics, the leading diagnostic company in the country with a workforce of close to 7,000 people. However, within a very short span of time of his joining, the erstwhile CEO left the company and the organization was technically without a CEO for about two months, operating through a steering committee. He was a part of a four-member steering committee and worked closely with the chairman and the board.

Eventually, Arindam got the coveted post of CEO in early March 2016. He believes that the reason he got the role was because of what he chose 'to do' and chose 'to be' at that point in time. He worked on many different fronts to make sure the employees stuck together, and the company made progress. Following are the few things that he worked on.

- *The big picture:* Overall, the attrition rate of the company was about 30 per cent, and within sales the percentage went upwards till 50 per cent. To make things worse, much of the senior leadership chose to part ways with SRL at the same time and there was a lot of scepticism in the air. People were worried about the sustenance of the organization. Arindam kept his cool in such a turbulent atmosphere and came up with a new organizational structure. He then worked with the other steering committee members, the Board and other stakeholders to implement the structure in the organization. He made sure that he did not just talk about his own function but the organization as a whole, just how a CEO would act. Through his initiatives, the organization found its much needed stability.

- *The organizational connect:* Arindam knew that since he was new to the organization, he needed to learn as much about the business as possible in the shortest possible time. His natural curiosity and a great appetite to learn came in handy, as he engaged with the field teams. He learned about the intricacies of the business as well as the prerogatives, difficulties, requirements of the people and teams. Armed with this knowledge, he was able to solve problems and find solutions.

- *The board connect:* There were different set of board members, namely, promoters, investors and the independent directors, each having their own world view. Arindam took pains to understand their perspective. He worked hard to make sure that his proposals addressed all their concerns.

- *The steering committee:* While leading the presentations, he made sure that all the steering committee members had a say and that all were engaged equally. He worked hard to build trust between members and made sure that he maintained transparency.

Arindam says, '*I took charge right from day one of the formation of the steering committee, thought like the CEO and made sure to take everybody along including those in the Steering Committee and the Board. My ability to step into bigger shoes and take people along helped me get promoted to the CEO position.*'

Arindam knows that a lot of quick changes happened in the last two–three years including his becoming the CEO, but he also realizes that it is a result of his efforts of the last 20 years. He adds, '*When one starts thinking about it, that is the way of nature. You plant a sapling and without your noticing, internal transformation happens in the plant and there comes a bud. And again, while nothing seems apparent from outside for a while, suddenly the flower blooms one day. The same is true of our efforts, we work hard for so many years and one day you see the results.*'

Why People Hesitate to Make Horizontal Moves?

Arindam believes there are quite a few reasons, but the major ones are:

60

- *'People think career is a straight-line journey or progression and they are always scared that if they make a horizontal move, they might lose two or three years of their professional life. This line of thinking is like that of a student who is afraid to change school in the middle of the academic year, afraid that his grades might suffer'.*

- *'People wrongly believe that skills and competence help them move up which obviously is not the case. The more senior you become, individual skills matter less and how you lead others becomes more important. I manage many people today who are far better in their skill sets than I could ever become. Sooner or later, dependence only on skill set leads to a career plateau. To be successful as a people leader, it is your EQ, more than your IQ that plays a significant role'.*

What Can Organizations Do?

Arindam believes 'performance' is something that keeps you in the role, gives you a good rating and helps to achieve some increments. But 'potential' is what moves you criss-cross up the ladder. High performance alone is not high potential. A high-potential person can be at low performance because of wrong fitment. The organization must recognize the potential and can facilitate a horizontal move and give the person a chance to perform.

The second thing the organization can do is to make sure that every high-potential person has a mentor. A mentor will challenge you to accept a difficult task and help you utilize your potential.

The third thing that the organizations can do is to provide experiences of alternate domains. Organizations that play an active role in career development of high potential people have more internal promotions and home-grown leaders.

Last thing is about building a culture that accepts horizontal movements as a norm. HR must make sure that dialogues between leaders and their teams happen during appraisals and regular performance discussions. Diverse experiences and successes in multiple domains should be recognized and rewarded to inspire others to seek horizontal movements.

How Does He Mentor His Own Team?

As a CEO, he sets the stage for the whole organization. He is actively involved and invested in his direct reports. They get into discussions on near and medium-term motivations including how can they achieve more, impact more, while not moving away from their core interests.

He thinks that the true purpose of the company and what difference it is bringing onto the sector matters a lot more than sales and profit. He appeals to team's core motive to keep them engaged. When they get the opportunity, they always come out with better ways of getting things done.

What Arindam Says about Your Next Promotion

'*For all mid to senior-level managers, it is important to first understand that if you are on a plateau or a table top, it is not a bad thing. Sometimes people beat themselves up for*

Message for Millennials

Arindam believes that millennials are a far more confident lot, with less baggage of past, and are also free of the scarcity mentality the older generation came with. Thus, horizontal growth should come more naturally as the order of the day to the millennials. His advice to them would be to seek new challenges at work and look for meaningful work and a solid learning curve. And nothing promises them more of such learning than a horizontal movement in career. A vertical growth teaches you 'more of the same', while a horizontal move meets their need for novelty.

this situation which is not right. A plateau is higher than plains with a nice overall view. You have already achieved something. Therefore, you should take cognizance of the fact that you are not at the bottom of the pile. It is a place where you can rest a bit before you start the next phase of your journey.'

'Second, drawing an analogy if you are physically on a plateau, you have to get down before climbing a higher peak. Sometimes, you have to traverse a valley too. It is nigh impossible to jump from one peak to another. The same is true when you are on a professional plateau. You have to be willing to come down, which means forgetting about your past achievements and preparing and learning about the new role as if you are a novice, putting in the hard yards and working your way up again.'

Arindam believes that if you have confidence in yourself and are ready to step up to new challenges, you can continue to gain new skills and broaden your horizon. When the time comes for the next big jump, you will be more than ready to assume the position, and nothing can stop you from your next promotion.

****

HORIZONTAL GROWTH: A TABOO?

You may have seen from the story that the horizontal moves were critical for Arindam and in hindsight his career path now looks very logical and complete. Despite a very clear logic and applicability of horizontal growth, it is still a bit of a dreaded zone. Given a chance, would you like to make a side move, if all was going well for you? If you knew that within two years you can get to the next level, would you rather stay in your current role and continue to sharpen your skill so that you get that promotion within your own domain. Would you not continue to do this over and over, till you reach the point of no return? Is this not how some people find themselves on a 'Career Plateau'? Many horizontal moves today are orchestrated by dire need to change when there is no other option or are mandated by one's leader or mentor. Let us have a look at what might be stopping you?

Everyone Imagines a Ladder

In a traditional growth story, everybody wants to take the position of their manager. The self-achievement is directly related to the next step on that ladder. You do your best, and you get to take your manager's role. Seems straight and the simplest career path. All you have to do is to learn to do better, perform the best among the team and you win.

Perception of Other People, Especially Peers

People may think that you were not going to get promotion within the group and that is why you sought to change. Your ability to deal with the perception of other people inhibits any move that works against the norm.

Fear of Unknown

You already know the stuff you do and when you grow to the next role, you will still be using a lot of it. You still are in your comfort zone. Your knowledge, your relationships will all be still in place and they will come to your aid. If you take horizontal growth, you can be working in a totally new area, you may need to learn much more, you may have to build new relationships and initially you may fail to even meet expectations. You will be working with quite a few unknowns. The fear of these unknowns is a great deterrent.

Loss of Personal Capital

If you move out, you will lose the personal capital you have built, and someone else from the team will take your place. He/she may progress faster than you and you may be set back in career a bit, compared to them. This is again like the story of career paths of Mary and Jasmine in the previous chapter. In the short run, Mary seemed to be on faster career path, but then Jasmine is able to overcome the hurdle of the plateau.

Question of Self-confidence

Do you have confidence in yourself that you can succeed in a new area? You may have your own doubts and that may hold you back. Do you have someone else who has confidence in you? A mentor or a guide or a coach? Someone who has vested interest in your growth, someone who can see in you what you cannot see in yourself? If not, this may also hold you back, and you may not make the right horizontal moves and may not achieve your full potential.

Opportunities

There may be lack of opportunities in your current environment and you may be needed to actively seek them out or make them happen.

If you always chose only vertical growth, it could limit your perspectives whereas enough horizontal experiences help you gain the skill to see the bigger picture in the complex and volatile corporate environment. This is a highly valued skill in the leadership and is the one that can be a differentiator. Do not let the minor hurdles hold you back.

WHAT CAN YOU DO?

It all begins with deciding to make a change. It is never too late. If you are on the plateau, I guess the time is now. Or was it yesterday? Like Arindam said, what happens in nature happens in real life as well and that after you have enjoyed the view from the plateau you are on and are ready to reach the next heights, you may have to step down and take that trail that leads to the next higher peak. You may have to take many such tours/de-tours to reach your destination. So, let us get started.

Seek Complimentary Experiences

You learn through specific job assignments and projects. And you must seek assignments that broaden your perspectives and add capabilities. The simplest could be to join cross-functional groups that work on multifaceted problems. One example is the digitization of businesses, such projects impact all the areas and engaging in them may be very useful.

Challenge Your Beliefs

Come out of your comfort shell and tell yourself that 'easy now' may be 'difficult tomorrow'. Seek more challenging tasks and stretch to achieve them. Fail early and fail fast and treat these opportunities to gain experiences.

Embrace Ambiguity

Do not be shy to take up relatively ambiguous projects and roles. Sometimes new positions or projects are created with good intentions but limited details. There are goals but no clear path. These roles give you an opportunity to build your own vision and pursue it. It will show the leadership that you are ready for the bigger roles.

Seek Help

When in doubt, reach out to your mentors and sponsors. They would have seen some of the situations that you may be grappling with and may provide the right guidance.

Unleash Your Potential

Believe in your heart that you have the potential. Do not let the lack of opportunity stop you. Take initiative and add value to other teams where you can. Use these side projects to unleash your potential. Sooner or later your initiative will get noticed and more people will seek to engage you. This may mean extra work for some time, but it will give you the horizontal exposure that is essential for long-term growth.

TRANSFORM YOUR MINDSET

A fixed mindset person will look at 'horizontal' move as a roadblock for growth of his/her career whereas somebody having a growth mindset will look at this as a growth opportunity and will look forward to it. The fact is that any role that provides you with an opportunity to learn is a growth opportunity.

FIXED MINDSET	GROWTH MINDSET
I know my area and I can do more here only.	I would definitely learn from the new area of work.
This is not the growth I was looking for.	It is a great opportunity to learn.
I am threatened.	I am being offered a new challenge.
Management has given me this role to keep me away from promotion.	Management has given me this role to broaden my horizon.
This is just going to be extra work for no extra pay.	This will help me unleash my potential.

HORIZONTAL GROWTH: IN ACTION

These few questions will help you reflect on the strategy for your own horizontal growth.

1. What are the three fields/areas of your expertise till now?

2. How relevant is your skill set to the today's world?

3. How relevant is your skill set to the future world based on your knowledge?

4. How ready are you for the future demands?

5. Name three roles that you would want to do in next five years.

6. How ready are you for these roles?

7. Identify the skills that you need to develop.

8. What horizontal moves can make you more ready for the future?

9. Who can help you make these Horizontal moves?

10. Do you have your successor ready for your current role?

11. Think about things that may stop you from the horizontal movement?

12. Who can help you overcome these hurdles?

13. How confident do you feel to make the horizontal move?

> One thing's for sure. If we keep doing what we're doing,
> we're going to keep getting what we're getting.
> One definition of insanity is to keep doing the same
> thing and expect different results.
>
> **Stephen R. Covey**

REFERENCE

1. Glassdoor. *Reviews on Glassdoor*. Available from: https://www.glass door.com/Reviews/Employee-Review-Google-RVW16055763.htm [Accessed 14th February 2020].

5

IMPACT BEYOND BOUNDARIES

66 99

*It is important to ask yourself why you're doing
what you're doing and what purpose it serves in
the big picture.*

MILEY CYRUS

Have you heard about Harvey Mudd College in Claremont California? It is an undergraduate college of engineering with a difference. They have been rated No. 1 College *for Undergraduate Engineering Program* by *US News* (2019)[1] and they have also been rated No. 1 in *Highest Mid-Career Salaries, PayScale's 2019–20 College Salary Report.*[2] You might wonder what makes them different? They have just one engineering major and do not offer a specialization unlike most of the other colleges. So why are their graduates earning more money? Why do organizations hire these engineers? Let us have a look at their philosophy about engineering.

'The engineering program philosophy is adopted to produce generalists, able to communicate across disciplines through the use and understanding of mathematics and systems-based analysis, who can design effective and innovative solutions to discipline specific problems. Our goal is to graduate students capable of solving real problems that span multiple engineering disciplines.'[3]

They heavily rely upon the fact that most of the problems are multidisciplinary and we need people who can cut across these disciplines to help find effective solutions. And I believe this is true for most of the problems we face today at our organizations. Rarely will there be problems that can be effectively solved within one vertical and rarely can we make change in one functional area without affecting many other interdependent functions.

RISING ABOVE SELF-DEFINED BOUNDARIES

There exist many boundaries within the work environment and people get used to working within these boundaries. But there are times when one must cross these boundaries to address the problems that span across them. The candidates at senior level are expected to create an impact beyond boundaries. Leaders are expected to understand the larger vision of the organization and rise above individual agenda by

1. Co-creating and collaborating with peers

2. Volunteering for various causes on behalf of the organization and so on.

In essence, the need to work across boundaries relates to collaborating and co-creating with other entities or groups both internal and external to help develop and grow the organization. In the VUCA world, the organizations must be able to continuously adapt to survive.

Consider an executive in sales who wants to improve customer satisfaction. Can the sales department alone take responsibility of improving customer satisfaction? And is the improved customer satisfaction the goal of just the sales team? Who else does he/she needs to involve? What are the key factors that affect customer satisfaction? Expertise of the sales staff? Quality? Cost? Delivery? Ease of ordering? Payment terms? Demo/Installation? Trainings? Ease of operating? After sales support? and so on.

Who can really own this project?

You are right! We must form a cross-functional team to look at this complex problem, no single department can achieve this on their own. Yet this one metric can make or break the entire organization. This is just one example of such type of projects. Let me give you some more examples.

- Enhancing the brand perception of the organization

- Improving partner experience

- Improving shareholder value

- Digital transformation and automation initiatives

- Diversifying product portfolio

- Geographical expansion and so on

The senior leadership have the responsibility of all such multidimensional projects. Would they like to work with people who have a narrow mindset or knowledge just of their own domains?

Again, you are right! They would want to have people, who can cross the boundaries, understand the big picture and make things happen.

CHALLENGES OF WORKING ACROSS BOUNDARIES

With respect to the example above, what happens when you try to meet the objective of customer satisfaction, can one department independently improve customer satisfaction without affecting other areas? Suppose we invest in 'after sales support' area to make improvements, we hire more people and train people to deliver better experience. Does that not increase our cost? If the cost increases a lot, this will lead to customer dissatisfaction. So, the person who manages the cost will be against any investments, if he/she does not cross the boundaries and understand the complete problem. If people work as a team, they might come up with a proposal that may involve some automation, that will result in a one-time cost increase but overall will result into a lower-cost structure and improved 'after sales support'. This may result into a significant improvement in customer satisfaction while achieving both objectives.

In case each individual group sticks to their own departmental objectives, we may not be able to make progress. The biggest challenge for people who work across boundaries is to remain open-minded about solutions. If one has preconceptions and is not open to discover new ways of getting things done, one may get stuck. You must be open to understand the nuances of other functions, understand the objectives that they carry and see them in the light of the overall project that they are working on. You need 'Big Picture' as well as 'Individual Context'. The person who works across the boundaries has to make 'We' from 'Me' and 'You'.

THE BIG PICTURE VIEW

Let me tell you about one of the teams that I worked for within an IT organization in the early days of my career—we were an unsuccessful team. Most of the team members were clear about their roles, but they did not care about how their work impacted the whole product. They just cared about their work and did not want to adapt to others. Once they had built their piece, they wanted others to make changes if required to make the whole system work. We all were living in separate black holes. In the end we all failed. The leader of the team could not set the right expectations or the right culture. I realized the difference when I started working for another leader for a different project which worked great. That leader made each responsible for the whole and made sure that we all understood this. He made sure we understood the big picture and our own role in it.

The important thing required for impacting beyond boundaries is the 'big picture view'. We can all see the picture for our own teams and fix any problems within our teams. But the trick to growth is to think beyond your area of work, to understand the picture beyond what you or your teams are responsible for. No one can win alone. You must demonstrate your value by making a genuine impact.

Now let us look at the story of a leader who created impact beyond boundaries.

****

DR TAPAN SAHOO: LET YOUR IMPACT BE FELT

Dr Tapan Sahoo is an electrical engineer from University College of Engineering in Odisha, one of the well-established government colleges. This story is about his journey from being a Graduate Engineer Trainee to becoming the Executive Vice President at Maruti Suzuki India Limited.

Tapan says, '*Impact beyond boundaries can be defined at different levels, impacting beyond one's core domain area, impacting beyond one's function, impacting beyond one's vertical within the organization, impacting beyond own organization as well as impacting beyond own Industry. And I feel humbled and blessed for being provided the opportunities to Impact beyond boundaries at all these five levels in my career at Maruti.*'

He believes you cannot create an impact without having the right attitude and aptitude. Attitude makes you look for change, and aptitude gives you the ability to make that change. And these must extend beyond yourself, your whole team must have the right attitude and aptitude. Tapan believes in the time-tested 4D mantra—Desire, Determination, Dedication and Discipline. He says that desire is the intent to make an impact and it is the initiation of the process, determination is the willingness to put extra effort to make that happen, dedication is following through to make sure you do not lose track and discipline makes sure that it is not a one-time effort and that you plan and execute in a timely manner.

There are many more such mantras in snippets from his journey that are surely going to impact you.

A Child's Desire to Make a Difference

Tapan recalls his childhood and the days when he studied in a village and describes how he was always keen on finding ways to improve his situation. When he was in 9th class, he developed a machine to help farmers sow paddy, which he later exhibited at a government organized science exhibition. He always had in his mind, a desire to help others, to improve the situation and help the society in general. This desire is what drives him to go beyond the boundaries to create a greater impact.

Forging His Own Path

In 1991, he got selected into Maruti through an all India Exam. He was one of the five electrical engineers in the batch, while 55 others were mechanical engineers. That number ratio made him wonder about the application of electrical engineering at Maruti. When the new hires were put through various trainings on electrical aspects, he realized that his future was likely to be in 'maintenance'.

He wanted to be in R&D and aspired to contribute in the field of design, he says, '*I always wanted to use my knowledge and creativity to make a difference*'. He sought a meeting with the head of engineering to share his interest in joining R&D. Based on the guidance he received, he pursued his case and finally joined the engineering department. Dr Krishan Kumar, the Quality Guru of Indian Auto Industry became his mentor and guide and he further adds,

'I do owe a lot to Dr Kumar, who was the head of Engineering and subsequently became a director in the board of Maruti, for his support and guidance through a large part of my career. He helped me in laying a very solid foundation for my career at Maruti.'

Creating the First 'Impact'

In 1992, Tapan and two mechanical engineers were called for a meeting by Dr Kumar. At that point, Maruti was in early stages of establishing R&D centre in Gurgaon. Dr Kumar was highly customer focused and wanted the young engineers to set up a few test rigs to simulate the problems the customers reported in the field and help identify the cause. Tapan says, *'It is believed in engineering that in case you are able to replicate a customer problem in the lab, you will be able to find the root cause and fix the issue.'* The enthusiastic young engineers got a clean slate and they freely painted on it. They figured their own way out, borrowed various jigs, fixtures and so on and the experimental set-up was ready in 1993.

They did various simulations and were able to replicate issues. One of the examples of simulations he mentions is that of the car's horn. The same horn that worked in Japan for the life of the vehicle failed in India in much shorter duration. When they simulated this in the lab, they found two key differences. First being that Indian drivers need to use the horn a lot more, which was very different from Japan or Europe or USA for that matter. The second was the environment—the temperature and humidity in India was quite different too. They were able to pinpoint the child parts that required improvement for Indian usage conditions.

As time progressed, Tapan wanted to be in the mainstream engineering and go beyond recreating failures. So, they met Dr Kumar and asked him for an opportunity to participate in design and they were then attached to various design groups. This was when they started participating in the full cycle, from simulating failures, to finding root cause, to writing down the revised standards for the products. Under the able guidance from seniors, Tapan started working with a few suppliers to get some early prototypes made for his suggested designs. The mentoring received by Tapan in those early days taught him to go beyond his scope, understand the big picture and contribute to the success of the organization.

When the new designs for the horn were implemented, you will be surprised to note that these three engineers and their lab helped to reduce the failures of horn in the field by 8,000 per cent. Such is the power of skill applied in the right way.

Deepening the 'Impact'

Tapan recalls early experiences of being called into meetings when Dr Kumar discussed the issues with the technical directors and CEOs of the suppliers. He would call Tapan and ask him to explain the problem details. Tapan got a chance to have one-on-one conversations with top management of the suppliers. This early exposure and empowerment were really enriching.

In 1995, he got an opportunity of four and a half months of design training in Japan. In addition to design, he learned the practices, processes and systems of Suzuki and established a connect with the Japanese team. He also learnt Japanese language skills, which helped him to make easy conversation.

In 1997, about six years into his career, with a desire to enhance his skills and knowledge, he enrolled into IIT Delhi for the MBA program. What really attracted him to the program was a unique specialization, that is, combination of strategy and technology. It was tough as he chose to continue with his job and opted for an evening study program.

Meanwhile, the lab team was getting to play a bigger role in the organization. The impact of the reports produced by Tapan's lab team grew when they started sharing them with supply chain and quality assurance departments. They became a great source of useful information and resulted into changes and improvements. Then the team set up the review processes including review meetings with the delivery teams. This further strengthened their role and helped deepen the impact—now they were making sure that the organization took advantage of the knowledge that was being generated in their test labs.

Gaining Diverse Experiences

In 2002, head of engineering informed him that as per new HR policy, Tapan must move to an adjacent function to gain diverse experience in the organization and continue to develop a sense of the bigger picture. Tapan joined Supplier Quality Assurance (SQA) team.

He quickly realized that the role was quite different. He was used to working at his own pace, defining his own plan and agenda and executing things in a phased manner. SQA was a front-end job. His role was to make sure that the products meet the specifications and resolve any issues raised by the production teams. There were thousands of parts and over the period of next three years he faced multiple issues that kept him on his toes. It was really a high-pressure time, there was a new regulation and he was in the middle of a huge effort by Maruti to develop and re-tune large number of components by working closely with the suppliers in about eleven months.

To further enhance his skills, in 2003 he enrolled for PhD. This was a time that tested him thoroughly and made him ready for his next big impact.

Impacting beyond Organizational Boundaries

After a successful stint in SQA, in 2004 he came back to engineering as the head of the electrical department. Tapan recalls that this was a time of great change in the industry '*That was the time when things started to change in the auto industry in India from technology perspective as well as from competition perspective. There were a lot of new features that were being introduced and the role of electronics in automobile was increasing.*'

He wondered how the auto industry, that was dominated by mechanical expertise, would deal with this drastic change. Tapan realized, as the head of electrical department, that he was leading an area critical to Maruti's success. He proactively raised the issue with the then head of Engineering Mr I. V. Rao. He built his case for the need of electrical expertise—looking beyond his function, his vertical as well as his own organization—he was looking at the whole ecosystem including the suppliers. He explained that while engineering department still had some electrical engineers, the rest of the value chain including the supply chain, the QA, the suppliers and so on were completely lacking the electrical expertise. He was convinced that within next 10 years the demand from this area will increase many folds and that the organization needed to start taking steps in that direction.

Mr I. V. Rao took it up with the joint managing director and an organization-wide movement started. Every year, from that point onwards, each department looked to hire more electrical/electronics engineers. Today, each function has many electrical and electronics engineers. Looking back, this is one big impact beyond boundaries that Tapan created and his actions helped Maruti to create a base for carrying out R&D activities in this domain.

During the days when he was heading the electrical engineering department, he got multiple opportunities to create an impact. Once, while reviewing the specifications of a component, he realized that tolerance specified was causing issues in the performance of the overall vehicle. Because Tapan understood the adjacent areas and was able to connect the dots, he made a minor modification in the specifications, which resulted in much better performance and much higher customer satisfaction for Maruti. The suppliers initially resisted the change because it meant additional investments on their part, but he asserted his claim with proper facts and logic and was able to drive the change.

As his team's impact grew, he started planning the expansion. He did not limit the focus purely on the Maruti's requirements in India but expanded the scope to include the potential requirements from Suzuki Japan. He believed that because of the unique talent pool in India, he could get people with electrical, electronics and even software skills that could easily complement the efforts of Suzuki Japan. He started with hiring a few engineering graduates and arranged training for them in Japan. This pool of engineers started to work for both India and Japan.

Tapan now faced a different challenge, he needed to scale up from a small team to a large one and quickly. He had to put his PhD on hold and focused completely on work. He worked on long-term strategy in terms of where he would see his team, what kind of profiles and roles he needed. Till 2007, he worked on getting the right people and grooming them. He realized that he needed people who could independently handle the operational aspects of the department so that he could focus on the long-term goals that will impact his organization in a bigger way. In 2007, he parallelly started to work on the PhD again and completed it in 2010. Meanwhile he had also started engaging with Society of Indian Automobile Manufacturers (SIAM) on the future of automobile industry. The discussions on electric vehicles and many other industry-related changes had started.

In 2012, the department grew into a division and he became a division head. He started representing Maruti at various industry fora and helped shape the future of the industry. For next three years, 2012–2015, Tapan worked with SIAM and Department of Heavy Industries while contributing to an important government policy called the National Electric Mobility Mission Plan 2020.

Broadening the Horizon

In 2015, the head of engineering, Mr C. V. Raman, spoke to Tapan and proposed another change. He said that Tapan had spent a lot of time in electrical, and that they wanted him to look at another important part of automobile development, that is, powertrain design. Tapan had learned a bit about engines in his college time but that was all the exposure that he had. He took this in his stride and after spending 24 years at Maruti, he set to learn about the heart of the automobile, the engine.

He spent next two years in the powertrain. He learned and saw things from a different perspective. He says, '*When you work for electric or electronic systems, you work a lot in imagination. No one can see electrons or current, but you make things that use them. However, in powertrain, everything is mechanical, so physical aspect was very important.*' He acknowledges the importance of the knowledge he gained while performing that role. He believes that it was an opportunity given to him to become well versed with a critical part of the organization and prepared him for the future roles.

In 2017, he moved into his current role heading the Product Planning, Design, Cost and Program Management. He believes he has had a phenomenal learning opportunity in his career. He has always believed in using his knowledge to create a positive impact on the organization.

Creating a Positive Spiral

Tapan believes that organizations are an ecosystem and that people are interdependent. If you create the impact beyond the boundaries, you can create a positive momentum, not just for yourself but also for others in the organization. If you do it right and create a positive engagement, others will also gain from it and would want more of the same, creating a positive spiral. He, however, cautions that you must make it a win-win situation for all involved, you must tread carefully and always respect the domain expertise of others. You must not cross the lines in your enthusiasm to create an impact. You must respect each other's roles and make the effort to take all along. You should not hog the limelight and make sure that you are able to help the other people involved, to shine in the process and become better in their own domains.

As each one of us may be very busy in our own domains, sometimes it will be difficult to find the time to do the extra effort required to deliver the impact beyond boundaries. He calls this extra effort— 'Plus Alpha'. You have choice, you can either limit your work to your 'sphere of control' or make the 'Plus Alpha' effort to widen your 'sphere of influence' and widen your own perspective. If you happen to travel to a new city for work, you may either just focus on the work and come back or you can make an effort, get up early in the morning to visit that famous temple in the city, get to work early and spare some time in the evening to walk on the beach. The 'Plus Alpha' effort will create these new experiences for you and let you explore the city and improve the overall quality of your visit.

What Can Organizations Do?

Organizations must encourage people to create an impact beyond their own self. The first thing that they can do is to set up formal or informal task groups or cross-functional teams to address multifaceted problems. If the organizations continue to set up such teams, each time there is a problem that needs attention from more than one function, people will start taking that as a way of life. They will volunteer for such teams, establishing a culture of 'Impact beyond boundaries'. The culture needs to be then carefully curated and supported. Organizations must encourage people who make the 'Plus Alpha' effort.

He again gives credit to Dr Kumar, who was a visionary and way ahead of his times when he initiated cross-functional teams to solve problems that were multifaceted. These cross-functional teams were a great place to learn about adjacencies and gain different perspectives. He also says that he is grateful to Mr Rao and Mr Raman for their guidance and support. In organizations, leaders need to provide right opportunity to people for an overall exposure and broadening their horizon. Tapan recalls another experience from his days in engineering when he was part of a cross-functional team that was set up to look at supplier development in a holistic manner. These were great learning opportunities and after each such initiative he was able to connect the dots a little better.

Tapan feels that organizations sometimes suffer from inordinate delays in projects. One of the contributing factors for such delays is that some of the tasks fall in the gaps between the 'functional domains'. This happens because of the way the organizational silos are created. If the organization can foster a culture of teamwork and create a few champions who can look beyond their own boundaries, the organization will run like a relay race, where people pass the baton to the next team before they taper off their own effort. They make sure that the baton is not lost in the process, they have the view of the full race and ensure that the organization wins. Tapan believes that creating a culture of 'impact beyond boundaries' helps improve organizational effectiveness.

How Does He Mentor His Team?

Tapan says that one of the ways that he mentors his people is to lead by example. He encourages the team to always look for the big picture and collaborate with various teams to help them contribute in the best way to meet the organizational objectives. He also shares with them the big picture and helps them connect the dots. He facilitates learning of adjacent areas for the team by encouraging them to participate in cross-functional projects.

What Tapan Says about Your Next Promotion

Tapan has been making steady progress in his career. He says, *'Promotion is basically recognition by the organisation that you have the potential and ability to take up the next role. Maruti recognizes talent for sure and gives you ample opportunity for growth and learning. And if you are able to learn, prepare for next level and do things which create a significant impact beyond the confines of your role and result into greater benefits for the organization, your growth is guaranteed. The organization will take care of your growth for you.'*

He believes that if you can create impact beyond boundaries, you also benefit a lot from the extra effort. Your scope starts growing, your recognition improves, leadership recognizes that not only are you good in your core area, you are able to contribute in other areas as well. Leadership will notice your abilities and consider you for role expansion, it could be a horizontal expansion or a vertical expansion. Tapan has a simple question for you, he says, *'If you just focus on what you are doing, how will you know that you are ready for the next role? Next role demands that you contribute in a bigger way and you need to be ready for it. You must create opportunities for yourself to experience other domains and contribute beyond your own limited scope.'*

Tapan further adds, *'Impact beyond boundaries can be defined at different levels and it happens step by step, you cannot just jump directly to next level without creating impact within your core area. You must understand your strengths and develop your core expertise. And then invest time and energy to also understand the adjoining areas and start joining the dots. You can only create the impact if you understand fully, "the big picture." And for joining the dots, you need to read, you need to understand and you need to interact with people. Then and then only can you create an impact worth reckoning.'*

Tapan also emphasizes on individual initiative. He recalls that as young engineers, when they started the lab, they could have limited themselves to testing, but when they were given an opportunity to search for components and create prototypes and so on, they enthusiastically picked up the additional scope, learned new things

Advice to Millennials

Millennials are very open minded, eager to learn, and ready to experiment. Tapan also notes that millennials love to solve challenges. Tapan's message to them is to be patient, conclude the task at hand before moving to the next 'interesting thing'. He also encourages them to volunteer for cross-functional task groups to create impact beyond boundaries from early days.

and created bigger impact. Tapan says, '*A lot depends on what you do with the opportunities you get.*' Another advice that Tapan has for people who want to make a difference is not to keep waiting for a formal opportunity to contribute. People must be ready to take up any opportunity that presents itself and engage with other people and find some common ground or shared goals.

Tapan believes that impact starts with the intention to contribute and to make a difference. The greater your contribution, the bigger your role will become.

****

WHAT IS STOPPING YOU?

It is normal to think in terms of 'My Team', 'My Department', 'My Approach', 'My Values', 'My Results' and 'My Challenges' and the next step is a natural extension to include your team and think in terms of 'Our Approach', 'Our Values', 'Our Results' and 'Our Challenges'. It is easy and it is very human, I guess. There is no trouble in this approach, except the boundaries you draw. Sometimes, you may draw boundaries too short, just so that you feel in control, because you want to be sure you can deliver what you promise. You close yourself up and avoid that difficult dialog with 'Others' and win in your own area while defeating the overall purpose of the project. It may be difficult to think beyond boundaries.

And yes, you are right, you must focus your energy on delivering your part of the responsibilities in the project and you must do justice to the metrics by which you are measured. But you must not stop short of doing the right thing even if that means you may have to challenge your metrics.

Let us look at a few thoughts that may stop you.

- I can only be responsible for my area.

- If they have a problem, they must sort it out on their own.

- I cannot make them successful at my cost.

- I do not have time to understand their work/process and I do not care.

- Why should I justify my approach? I already know the best for my domain.

- It will be tough to explain this to them, let me work out the best I can.

- They will not understand, why waste time in trying.

- It is a win-lose equation, all cannot win. I must win for myself.

- This is extra work and not the main task, I will allocate it the least time and priority.

- Many people tried this in the past and failed, I do not want to fail.

And so on. Each of these stems from the fact that you draw boundaries and consider yourselves responsible for stuff within your boundary. You need to think bigger than what you are doing but sometimes you are restricted by limiting thoughts.

HOW DO YOU CREATE IMPACT BEYOND BOUNDARIES?

There are two key suggestions for you. First one is about gaining the 'big picture' perspective and the second one is about helping others align with it. You will need others to work with you to create any positive impact beyond boundaries and creating common understanding and goals will take some effort.

Knowing the Big Picture

Start thinking from your leader's perspective. You would be able to see the big picture within your own teams and may be able to better collaborate with your peers.

You would need to do the following:

- Know about the adjacent areas, their objectives, their targets and their constraints

- Know about your leader's objectives

- Develop better working relationships with the peers

- Share progress and challenges with the peers

- Take active interest in their success

- Be ready for those constructive dialogues

- Be ready to accept change and adapt

- Talk for the whole department/organization, not just your own function.

You could benefit from the following:

1. Volunteering for some cross-functional teams

2. Believing in serving your customer from the core

3. Taking feedback from your mentor

4. A 360 survey to know about your ability to influence and impact others.

Creating 'We'

Well you understand, but the others do not. And, they may not have any incentive to spend time to understand your suggestions for joint initiatives. So, how do you go about doing things then? You must be able to take others along in this journey and you may not always have the authority to get things done. The following steps may help you achieve your objectives.

- *Start with the big picture:* Never start with what you need, start the dialogue with the why? You need to first make sure that everyone has a shared goal. Something that the others can relate to.

- *Stay simple:* Do not complicate with many 'what-if-scenarios' or scare people with dire circumstances and potential failures. State the objective and seek the support that you need.

- *Clarify:* Share your strategy and plan and make sure that you are able to clarify any doubts raised. Always link it back to the end goal. Make sure it is not perceived as something that will just benefit you or your department/function.

- *Stay open:* Stay open for the dialogue, no one wants you to fail. Listen to each suggestion and try and link it to the objective. You may have thought of one best way, but others can come up with even better ones. Adapt your plans to include others. Respect others to gain their respect. Value others to be valued yourself.

- *Track:* Track progress and share regular updates with stakeholders. Stay connected and be ready to have additional dialogue and change the course as necessary.

TRANSFORM YOUR MINDSET

A fixed mindset person will look at 'Impact Beyond Boundaries' as extra work, thankless job and a potential for failure, whereas somebody having a growth mindset will look at this as a growth opportunity and will look forward to it.

FIXED MINDSET	GROWTH MINDSET
I am fully occupied with my work.	I can add value.
What is in it for me?	How can I add value?
Why should I care about their area?	I can learn something new.
My metrics will be impacted.	It gives me an opportunity to transform.
This is a thankless job.	The organization needs this.

MAKING AN IMPACT: IN ACTION

These questions will help you reflect and figure out the strategy for contributing in projects that cross the boundaries.

1. What are your behaviours that stop you from collaborating?

2. What can you do about it?

3. What are the areas/projects where you can make an impact beyond your role?

4. What interests you the most?

5. How will it benefit you?

6. What could be the challenges?

7. Who can help you?

8. How can you collaborate with other people on the project you chose?

9. How will such an initiative impact the big picture?

10. How will it help you evolve your team and improve the contribution of your team to the organization?

Great things in business are never done by one person; they're done by a team of people.

Steve Jobs

REFERENCES

1. Harvey Mudd College. *Harvey Mudd ranked no. 1 for undergrad engineering.* Available from: https://www.hmc.edu/about-hmc/2018/09/10/harvey-mudd-ranked-no-1-for-undergrad-engineering/ [Accessed 14 February 2020].

2. College Salary Report. *PayScale's 2019–20 College Salary Report.* Available from: https://www.payscale.com/college-salary-report [Accessed 14 February 2020].

3. Harvey Mudd College. *Program accreditation.* Available from: https://www.hmc.edu/engineering/program-accreditation/ [Accessed 14 February 2020].

6

RELATIONSHIPS THAT MATTER

" "

Earn trust, earn trust, earn trust. Then you can worry about the rest.

SETH GODIN

Relationships matter to everybody at work. Being an Executive Coach, I have had the opportunity to listen to multiple stories of how people connect at work. We all have been part of good and not-so-good relationships, conflict situations, misunderstandings and so on. We have suffered the consequences of conflicts resulting from poor relationships and mistrust.

Organizations have always appreciated the importance of relationships with customers. They invest a lot in creating, cultivating, developing and maturing these relationships. Relationships play a big role in any sale. For every complex sale, the salesperson must first establish a deeper connect with the buyer. Ninety per cent of the organizations say that they will buy from someone they trust.[1] Having trust in relationships will also get you access to right resources for effectively delivering on your assignments. They also get you a 'listening ear' to share your thoughts and a chance to influence the stakeholders. If you have strong bonds with someone, you prefer to work with them even if there are many others with equal qualifications or offerings. If you have a great connect with someone, it is easier to have the difficult conversations with them, because there is a mutual trust already.

RELATIONSHIPS AT WORK

Relationships are important for growth at work beyond the first stage of contribution. Once you move beyond 'contributing dependently', you need to build your own connects at work to perform effectively. The impact of relationships grows as you move to next stages of contribution.

If you desire to get to the top management, the path lies through some key decision-makers. In the good old days of vertical growth, the path was a straight one and you built your relationships as you went about doing your work, collaborating with others and contributing in a positive way through your work. You almost always had the relationships you needed. And as you stepped into new roles, you leaned on your existing relationships to gain new ones. You were always in touch with people that you would be working for or working with; there were seldom any surprises. And people outside of your close circle did not matter much. But as the organizations become highly matrixed and adopt flatter structures, you need to develop relationships beyond your function even for regular business. Your growth will most likely be impacted if you do not have the right relationships.

WHO KNOWS 'WHAT YOU KNOW'?

Do you remember, how many people interviewed you before you got your current job? If you belong to one of the hierarchical organizations, you might say 'two' or maybe 'three', one hiring manager, one HR person and maybe one skip-level manager. But if you belong to a new age organization, you might say five or more, HR manager, hiring manager, a potential colleague or two and even one person from the team that will report to you plus some more. Have you wondered why?

As discussed in the previous chapters, quite a few successful organizations now have a much flatter organization structures and others are following them at an increasing pace. There is no career ladder anymore, it is a career mesh, or a career lattice or a career maze. It is not only difficult to get in, but also difficult to navigate. You may sometimes wonder which way will lead you 'Up'.

So, how does one navigate for growth. Well beyond a point in career (and that point is somewhere in mid management), 'Who Knows What You Know?' matters more. If you know a lot and can achieve wonders, but the CXOs do not know, they are likely to hire someone else for the position that you have been seeking all along. CXOs are key influencers for any hiring in top management and they lay a lot of emphasis on the confidence they have on the candidates. Confidence begins with familiarity and shared connections. So, nurturing these relationships is an absolute key to getting those roles that you desire.

DELIVERING SUCCESS IN NEW AGE ORGANIZATIONS

In highly matrixed and relatively flatter organizations, the resources are quite spread, with different teams having access to a part of the organizational capability. You could either be responsible for a project or you could be having a team that is spread across various projects as contributing members.

In the first case, you are responsible to deliver a project with a bunch of professionals, who report to your peers and sometimes even much senior leaders. You need to have the right relationships with the managers of your team members to make sure that

- They give you the time to explain your project and share progress and raise any relevant concerns.

- They provide you with a resource who has the right skills to make your project successful.

- They provide the right guidance to their team member when the team member needs support for complex tasks on your project.

- When things go wrong and you have a conflict with the team member, you can get the support of their managers to resolve it.

- When your team identifies additional resources required, you can reach out to the right stakeholders and make your case.

If you do not have the right relationships, you need to do a lot of up and down within the organization just to make sure that you have the right team and that the team has access to all the right resources and that they are allocating the right amount of time and energy on your project.

In the second case, when you are the one who is providing resources to various projects, your team members represent you in those projects. Any positive or negative feedback is a reflection on your work. It will be better if you had the relationships with all the stakeholders, so that you can get more details, compared to what your team member may be able to comprehend and share with you. That way you can get the holistic view of the project, its progress, the challenges it faces and the interactions between the teams. If you do not have the right connects, people may hesitate to proactively share some feedback and you may not be able to address issues before they become big.

You also need to make it a better experience for your team, while producing great results for the organization, but how do you do that? A big project may demand the best resource despite the fact that the skills of your best guy may be more suitable to another project. So how do you navigate these situations? Relationships and past credentials backed with your personal commitments may be able to help you provide a less experienced resource for the big project, because that is what is needed.

Another important part is getting recognized for your efforts. Your team member has provided critical support to a project, but it was not acknowledged by the stakeholders. No one knows how much work your team is putting in. If you have the right relationships, the stakeholders will acknowledge the work done by your team and make sure that you get your due credit. That way you can show the value your team brings to the table.

BUILDING CONNECT WITH YOUR TEAM

Leaders are expected to always produce the best products and services despite the ever-changing environment. Traits like innovation, problem-solving, decision-making and strategy cannot be the responsibility of the leader alone. The entire team must contribute towards achieving the bigger picture, and simultaneously excelling at their own scope or part. In this constantly changing world, great teams continue to outperform the market. It is the leader's responsibility to develop and engage teams in such a way that they always come out as winners. However, there are many instances, where teams are not performing their best and leaders suffer because of it. Your team is critical to your success. The need of the hour is for the leaders to take their people along as they work at high pace in an agile environment.

CONNECTING BEYOND ORGANIZATION

Your relationships beyond your organization also come handy when you are working on large projects of strategic importance to the organization. The information that you can collect informally through your connections can help validate the internal assumptions and sometimes provide the necessary course correction. Senior people value the 'resourcefulness' and the ability to contribute beyond your role. They take it as a sign of strength and would weigh it in your favour when considering a bigger role for you.

Imagine that your organization is going to get affected by a new policy and you happen to have the relationships with the consultant who is working with the government on the policy framework. The opportunity you can provide to your organization to contribute to that policy and get timely insights on the framework is priceless. Will your organization value you for it? I am sure it will.

Now let us look at the story of a leader who values 'people-connect' a lot and has been able to make great strides in his career starting from Army to the Global Tech world as well as Tech Start-up world.

****

KULMEET BAWA—A DIVERGENT LEADER: ON HIS TRYST TO MERGE THE ART AND SCIENCES

You are never given a wish without also being given the power to make it come true.

Richard Bach

The above quote has been a mantra to Kulmeet's philosophy towards life—both personal and professional. Clearly a divergent of sorts, he believes more than anything else in the magic of life, in living several lives within a lifetime. He consistently questions the 'Is', recharges himself through nature's mysticism and believes most of all, in the simplicity of life. Literature and poetry have always been close to his heart—often he can be found passionately quoting lines from 'Lochinvar' or throwing in an analogy from the *Merchant of Venice*, just in case he is not humming lines from Simon and Garfunkel's 'Sound of Silence'.

Kulmeet started his career in the Indian Army and excelled as a leader there. After spending 12 years serving the nation, he set out to explore the corporate world. He was at the frontline in the army and has been leading from the front in the corporate world too. With his unique ability to relate to people, he has learned to break barriers and build unbreakable bonds. He says, '*Be it the army or the Civvy Street, if people trust you, they will place their very lives in your hands. The onus of how you bring them home safely, now lies on you.*'

Kulmeet has always believed in writing his own story. He has left a trail of successes in his wake and is now on the path to create the next one. What follows are a few snapshots out of his playbook!

The Early Years

Kulmeet went to school in Delhi and Mumbai—his dad was a senior officer in the Indian Navy, and they shuffled between the two cities. Before being presented with the choice of going abroad for higher studies, Kulmeet took a decision to join the Indian Armed Forces, perhaps due to his father's influence. He left school after Grade 11 and joined the National Defence Academy (NDA) at the age of 16. Three years of military training at NDA followed by another year at the Indian Military Academy helped build leadership resilience and shaped the Kulmeet Bawa we know today!

He says, '*NDA was fantastic. The military training brought us down to mother earth or ground zero, made us humble. I will say that those years sort you out for life, because they build in you a strength that shapes your outlook towards life and helps ingrain leadership in its truest form.*'

He hated his first year at NDA because it was tough, and there was always so much happening in the Academy. He shares that initially he was petrified of jumping from what was a compulsory 10-meter board into the pool. It was a near death experience for him, as it was to many of the other cadets. It was basically the fear of what lies on the other side—the fear that the water would hurt. Once he had done it a couple of times, he realized that all he had to do was to overcome the fear which was merely in his head. The water or the pool could not hurt him—but the ghosts to be battled were the ones in his mind; the exercise like many others was designed to help cadets become stronger.

The Years at the Army

In 1990, at the age of 20, he got commissioned into '65 Armoured Regiment', one of the finest regiments of the Indian Cavalry. In the 12 years that Kulmeet served in the army, he was posted across the Indian subcontinent including an extended tenure in Jammu and Kashmir. At a very early age, he got the opportunity to serve as Aide-de-Camp to a veteran politician, Mr Mata Prasad, who was the governor of a North Eastern State. The tenure gave him a bird's eye view into the political and bureaucratic mindset, and it was in this stint that Kulmeet learnt the most about people and how the human mind works—an experience that groomed him for the years that followed.

In 1999, he joined the School of Armoured Warfare in Ahmednagar where he took up a dual responsibility, imparting knowledge on war related strategy as well as setting up the computer wing. It was here that he got exposure to information technology and in parallel, harnessed his skills around the Art of War!

Life could not have been better—a brilliant career with a clear path to progression! And then, Kulmeet's exploration bug surfaced. His hunger to learn and apply his skills to the world outside of the army was propelling him to do more. Perhaps the fact that he was doing well and had certainty in his career at the army also bothered him, since he was looking for more challenges.

He consulted his father and discussed the idea of leaving the army. Kulmeet says, '*I believe that each generation should make progress and achieve at least three times more than the previous. My father was already a very senior officer in the Navy, and I wanted to be able to achieve more with his guidance.'* After about a year's effort, Kulmeet was allowed to retire prematurely and the next stage of his career began.

Making Career Choices

When he came out of the army, he planned to pursue his dream of going to a business school. He visited a few schools including INSEAD, London Business School, Wharton and so on and then he came across ISB in Hyderabad, India and liked it. In 2003 he joined ISB, in one of its initial batches. The MBA program was a great learning and armed him very well for the transition into the Civvy Street.

He says, *'Statistics pointed to the fact that folks from the "armed forces" usually chose careers like logistics or security or HR. But I also recognized that the fastest way to make a difference would be to get into the business side and own both the top and bottom lines of a business. And I was willing to own the business risks and welcomed the adrenalin rush associated with high risk-high return scenario.'*

He fondly remembers the first offer he got. One of the global FMCG majors, after a few rounds of interviews, made an exception for him and offered him a lateral role of managing tea estates. When they asked if he would take it up, he said, *'Absolutely! And I would love to, but I will probably come back to you in a decade and a half for that role.'* He wanted his career to mirror the fast-paced growth he envisaged for the organizations that he would join. His subsequent meeting with Bhaskar Pramanik who was heading Sun Microsystems opened up a whole new door. He recalls one of the first questions that Bhaskar asked him that was, *'What is a cavalry officer doing outside the army?'* and he still remembers replying, *'Things were going too well in the army and I was looking for new challenges.'* Sun was at the cutting edge of the technology and appealed to Kulmeet as being in the forefront was important to him.

While FMCG had its own charms, Kulmeet chose to take up sales role in Sun Microsystems as he was intrigued by the potential of exploring the unchartered territory of technology. His ability to trust his guts has always held him in good state. In hindsight, Kulmeet realizes that he liked high speed action of working in high growth organizations and that he loved building businesses up from scratch. He has done that many times over.

Advent into Corporate Career

He managed his corporate career with a difference. Even when he was in the top leadership positions in Adobe he used to be known as an entrepreneur in a large company because he would run it like a small and agile organization. He truly believes that disruptive innovation is most critical in today's world and adds '*In today's day and age with the world becoming flatter, there are no solid lines of disciplines such as history, physics etc. The lines are blurring every day, and everything innovative is at the cusp of various disciplines of study. The fun begins when the art and science merge together and when creativity and neuroscience dovetail. If you can learn to combine disciplines and ride on simplicity of words, you can connect with people at a different level. You can then communicate your ideas effectively and I think you would be successful anywhere.*'

Kulmeet learned the nuances of a technology business very quickly. He understood the power of the customer and mastered being in their shoes and he was often able to know their problems even before they themselves realized. He was there to support and help them. In fact, he never thought of them as his customers. He would consider them all on the same team, with one goal, to make each one of them successful. Each project to him was like a mission, where he was responsible for his whole regiment, which included his team members and the customers together. He was never competing for their business; he was only helping them succeed. He naturally connected with people and left a deep impression upon them. He had seamlessly built a pool of deeply served relationships all around him!

In 2010, Kulmeet moved to Microsoft to lead their government and healthcare business. Microsoft was the shortest stint for Kulmeet, though he remembers it as fast-moving two years. He acknowledges that at Microsoft he got the opportunity to work with two great leaders he really admires; Karan Bajwa who was his leader at Microsoft and also his old mentor Bhaskar Pramanik who had joined Microsoft as the Chairman. He says, '*Microsoft was fun, but it was short. Though I was enjoying the work, when I saw the opportunity to make a difference with Adobe in India, I decided to move. It appealed to my greater calling to shape the company culture, craft the strategy and create a future that I had imagined.*'

In 2012, he left Microsoft and joined Adobe, transitioning to paint another success story, just like he had imagined. He spent seven and a half years at Adobe and grew from being head of enterprise sales to becoming the top man, leading India and South Asia business. He had some of the most amazing achievements of his career at Adobe. While Adobe grew phenomenally at a global level, India business grew exponentially and created history under Kulmeet's leadership.

Making the Next Big Difference

However, the hunger to build something new once again took over. Kulmeet's incessant yearning was to build a business grounds up by creating a vibrant culture and getting teams to work together to write history. His quest to leave a legacy got him into the start-up world.

He decided to join Resulticks which is one of the world's fastest growing truly omnichannel marketing automation platforms. He is now based out of Singapore and has taken up the role of COO and is involved in creating and executing their global strategy.

He is on a high as always, setting up and growing a new business, something that he is best at and has always enjoyed doing.

The Mantra of People and Relationships

Kulmeet believes that the transition from the army to the world of business has been very natural for him because he has been able to crack the basic code itself. He believes it is all about people and relationships. Leadership in the army is tough as it may involve life and death decisions for not just yourself but your whole team and the people that you are defending. You need to develop a deep trust and confidence in the people that you lead.

At times, Kulmeet may have been perceived as a tough leader because he has been responsible for driving both top line and bottom line growth for organizations as well as ensuring that its brand is always at its highest. However, while he sets a high bar for himself and others around him, he always ensures that his people come first. He believes in 'Being Firm, but Kind!'

He says, '*When you look at any facet of your daily life, whether it is customers, quarterly numbers, million dollars deals, or your teams, it is all about people. If you can get the people equation right, then everything else falls into place.*'

The People Equation

Kulmeet believes that if you can get into the other persons world by breaking down the shackles and understand what is happening on the other side, you can get relationships right. He believes that you must be transparent in your interactions. To build great relationships, you must learn to listen. He says you must not focus only on what is being said, you must also focus on the unsaid, since it is often the 'silence between the words' that matter the most.

His father inspired him a lot, he says '*I always saw him doing for people, it could be his juniors, seniors, relatives or friends. He was always warm and welcoming. He was a big influencer in my life, and he taught me that once you are connected with people, it is not about what you take from them, it is mostly about giving. It is about what you can give them.'*

Kulmeet explains from his personal experience that customers give business to you and not to the company. They trust the person in front of them. If you break their trust any time by failing on the deliverables, you must own the failure and act to serve them in the best possible way. He says, *'It is not that the people equation or relationships cannot go wrong sometimes, things can go out of hand, but you can always get them back on track by acknowledging the mistake and then taking ownership for corrective action.'*

Key Principles of the People Equation. The first and the most important principle has always been transparency and genuineness. Transparency invariably translates into credibility. And it is important irrespective of the relationship, that is, whether you are talking to your juniors, seniors or peers.

The second principle that has always worked for him is his passion for life. Kulmeet's passion is almost infectious and helps him energize, engage and connect with people in the right way.

The third principle is simply 'doing' for others and for the greater good. He believes that you need to invest in people because that in itself is satisfying and not because you may need something in return from them.

He has always been able to grow within the organization many times faster than the regular career pace. He says that your career advancement depends a lot on 'who you are'. Your brand is not just your passport within the organization, it extends to the entire industry and into all areas of your life, professional and personal.

Mistakes that One May Make in People Equation. He shares that one of the learnings he has had from a very early age is that you cannot have an agenda. When you are sitting and talking with someone, you need to be very conscious and cautious that you are not in there just for your selfish interest. If you try to build relationships with an agenda, it will always show up. You can only make a lasting relationship if you are genuinely interested in the people you meet and not just in the transaction you want to conduct with them.

Often in today's age, people interpret relationships and popularity to 'likes and comments' on social media. While you can definitely use and benefit from social media, Kulmeet does not think that bonds can be built through social media. They definitely require the human to human connect.

What Can Organizations Do?

Kulmeet believes that in every organization the tone is always set from the top. Leaders need to set the right examples by caring for people outside of just their professional context. Leaders must ensure that they build more leaders and strive for the success of the broader team. If they set the tone by keeping the customers and employees at the core of their actions, others will be able to sense the same and imbibe these values. These values will in turn be instrumental in building the culture for success and camaraderie.

How Does He Mentor His Team?

He says the best way to mentor people is to lead by example. He believes in creating a shared vision that is larger than life and then getting his teams to believe in themselves and what they are going after. His teams get to see him in action all the time, during meetings, offsites, conferences and during social engagements. He believes that this is the most effective way for him to inspire them.

As he said before, the tone has to be set by leadership. It is not about preaching or telling others how to do something. Teams learn a lot more when their leaders are exhibiting a specific behavioural trait.

What Kulmeet Says about Your Next Promotion

His advice to all professionals is to develop true relationships with people all around, with customers, peers and your teams—essentially expand your sphere of influence. You should be authentic at all times—even if it hurts. Success will automatically be yours at every step!

As a leader, Kulmeet wants you to really care about your people and your organization. It can never be about just a selfish interest, that is, a specific project or a desired outcome and so on. It is about connecting with people and more than them, their lives. He would like you to focus on making your people prosper and flourish. That cannot come from an agenda, it can come from genuine concern and empathy. Once you connect with people in the right way, all other things start automatically falling in the right place—engagement scores, orders, profits and so on.

You must remember that the culture always begins at the top. It must be set at the top, but at the same time has to be penetrated through mid-level managers in the right way. Passion, authenticity and genuineness is important. He keeps telling the leaders that they set the standards.

Message for Millennials

Kulmeet believes millennials are wired differently and their interpretation of relationship is very different in multiple ways and it is quite transactional. His suggestion to them is to have more depth in relationships and to invest in loyalty in those relationships.

People must learn something every day from you. What is it that they measure themselves against? What is their benchmark? They will stretch themselves based on the benchmark you set for them. As leaders we must set the bar high.

Kulmeet advises you to create the human bonds, for the greater reason to connect and serve. He believes that if you get the people connect right, your growth will happen for sure, probably faster than you assumed.

****

ROADBLOCKS TO BUILDING GREAT RELATIONSHIPS

Relationships are like the oil that keeps the engine in good shape and performing at the peak. If you forget to get this oil, you may still work, but it will be hard work with a lot of friction, and you will make slow progress. The progress will wear you off and you may not have the strength to keep fighting your way up to the top. Relationships are not incidental; they are a key thread in the fabric of success. If you lack these skills, make sure you are working on them.

There are tons of reasons that stop people from building great relationships at work. Have a look at a few listed here and see which ones you may relate to.

No Reason to Connect

Many times, we do not have a reason to connect with other co-workers. At work, you may consider it an overreach in case you connect with someone when you have no common assignments. You are afraid you may be wasting their time, or you might just leave a bad impression.

Past Experience

Sometimes you are competing with another person/team for access to same resources and whether you won or lost a specific case, it left a bad taste in your mouth and you like to avoid that person. Or you have collaborated in the past with poor results and see no need to continue the relationship. In short, the past experiences have created trust problems or there is a lack of mutual respect.

Lack of Personal Connect

In the virtual environments, you work with a lot of people remotely. Quite a few times you do not even connect a name with a face. For example, you may have exchanged emails and got a lot of support from Ben, but you are not aware who he really is and when he is visiting your office. You also are not aware of all the domains that Ben supports and have just interacted with him for a specific task. You do not know how else you can help each other and have not invested to connect at a deeper level.

Lack of Opportunity

Though you would not have minded building a relationship you did not get the chance. And you hesitated to create an opportunity on your own.

Hierarchy Barriers

The person is much too senior to you and you did not have the courage to connect. Or your seniors keep all such relationships to themselves and create a barrier for you.

Expectation of Returning Favours

Even if you could do something for a co-worker, you refrain from spending the effort because you know that the co-worker is in no position to return favours, so the effort may just be a drain on you. Or you do not ask for a favour because you believe you can give nothing in return.

WHAT CAN YOU DO ABOUT IT?

In addition to the good work you are doing in your current role, you should utilize every opportunity to build stronger bonds with people, always putting in the efforts to understand them at a deeper level. Let us have a look at a few ways to build strong bonds.

The 100/0 Principle

There is a book called *The 100/0 Principle* by AL Ritz.[2] It shares a great secret for building relationships. In summary, if you want to build great relationships with someone, you must find out more about their business and their objectives and then find a way to help them. You must do your 100 per cent without expecting anything in return. If you keep up with honest intensions, a bond will form, and the foundation of a lasting relationship will be built.

Find Common Grounds

You should find opportunities to interact and know others and connect with a wider set of people at work. For example, work on organizational projects that involve diverse teams such as improving customer satisfaction or employee engagement and so on. You could also be a mentor or seek a mentor, present at an industry forum and so on.

Understand Others

When you interact with people, you will gain a lot of perspective if you discuss beyond the task at hand. Understanding the people and knowing about their motivations and their problems will help you to offer your best support. Any support that you extend beyond your scope will be appreciated even more and will help you connect at a deeper level.

Be Respectful

As you interact with people from diverse backgrounds and regions, you will need to learn to respect their choices. If you show them that you care about their preferences, they will also make room for your choices and a mutual bond will build up.

Build Trust

Do what you say and build credibility. Keep your promises. If things change, keep everyone posted, no one likes surprises. If there are problems, stand together with people, work with them to resolve them. In general, do everything that you would want others to do to win your own trust.

Appreciate

Look for good in every person and every situation. Appreciate people for the good in them and the good work that they put in. Even when you have to convey the need for improvements, you should try and talk about the positives first. That will motivate people to do more and make them keen to listen to you.

TRANSFORM YOUR MINDSET

A growth mindset always helps you to be more open and receptive to building long lasting relationships.

FIXED MINDSET	GROWTH MINDSET
I do not have time to connect with people.	Let me work out options to connect with these people.
People have attitude.	People are different.
It is difficult to connect to different types of people.	Let me learn how to handle different people in the best possible way.

111

FIXED MINDSET	GROWTH MINDSET
I cannot trust them.	Let me give them a chance.
I had bad experience with that person in the past.	Future may not be same so I will evaluate new experiences as they evolve.

RELATIONSHIP BUILDING: IN ACTION

The following few questions will help you to reflect on your relationship building priorities.

- How good are you on relationships at work?

- What are your key strengths to develop relationships?

- What do you think you need to learn for developing relationships?

- Who are the key stakeholders you should have a connect with? (Write their names)

- How far their level is from your current level in the organization?

- Rate the quality of relationship with each one of them on the scale of 1 to 10.

- Do you understand the following about them?

  › Their aspirations and goals

  › Their communication styles

  › Any past experiences/resentments that needs to be solved before the relationship becomes better

  › How can you be of any help to them?

  › What are the three things you can do to strengthen the relationship?

> › How frequently do you meet them?

> › How can you be in contact with them more often in a genuine way?

> › What could be the challenge?

> › How could you overcome that challenge?

- What will you do to develop the areas you noted above for stronger relationships?

I believe that you can get everything in life you want if you will just help enough other people get what they want.

Zig Ziglar

REFERENCES

1. SalesForce Search. *3 Reasons why trust is so important in sales.* Available from: https://www.salesforcesearch.com/blog/httpwww-salesforce search-combid1563513-reasons-why-trust-is-so-important-in-sales/ [Accessed 14 February 2020].

2. Ritz AL. *The 100/0 Principle: The Secret of Great Relationships.* Naperville: Simple Truths.

7

CONVERSATIONS THAT MATTER

66 99

The art of communication is the language
of leadership.

JAMES HUMES

As part of our professional life, we have conversations all the time. The importance and the nature of conversations have changed though. From small cosy workgroups that remained stable for long, we have embarked upon a world where things change quite often. As business environments change and reorganizations happen every 12–18 months, you may need to work with people who are relatively new to you. You may not have the history on your side; they may not know much about you and vice versa. Conversations that you have with various people at work gains a new level of importance. These conversations will determine the success you will have together.

EARLY STAGES OF CAREER

In early stages of your career, the conversations are relatively limited to a close circle and rarely does one get the chance to have business conversations outside of your own function. That works out quite well for most of the people since just a few people matter. The tenures of the relationships are longer and building of mutual trust happens gradually. Personal bonds start developing as you move beyond work-related conversations. Over time, you develop stronger and deeper relationships with the people. If you lack the skill to have great conversations, you can still leverage your work, attitude, dependability and knowledge to build trust. And you can gain the skill of great conversations eventually.

MOVING UP

Beyond a certain level, the capability to have those clear and meaningful conversations become important in addition to your ability to work hard and produce results. The changes start when you work beyond a close circle of colleagues, when you start leading teams, when you are in cross-functional groups, in other words when you start becoming responsible for a group outcome and your own work is a small piece of the larger outcome. This is the time when you have many conversations to make things happen. The quality of these conversations matters a lot and how others perceive you and your motives will be the key. Communicating upwards also becomes an integral part of your work. You will have to share your ideas and progress with the leadership teams. How you conduct those conversations will have a lot of impact on where you can reach in your career.

You might have noticed that people who are better at conversations move faster in the organizations. They get promoted more often! It is not that they have the best performance individually, there could be others who are better, but the trick is that they know how to get things going. The main skill that differentiates them from others is the articulation, presentation and the ability to create conversations that can help move things forward. These people are not fixated, they are open-minded, and they look for solutions through these conversations. To build the grounds for great business conversations, they take time to connect with various stakeholders. They are good listeners too, and they make sure that others do have the chance to share their thoughts. They make things appear easier than they really are and can put people at ease. Others love to talk to them, and they emerge as leaders by default.

It is difficult to ignore this capability, sooner or later they get noticed and are usually given additional responsibilities or bigger roles and they surpass others in their organizations.

NEW AGE ORGANIZATIONS NEED MORE CONVERSATIONS

The world of new age organizations is more complex. We covered quite a few aspects of the flatter organizations in the first few chapters. Most of your work in these organizations is based on cross-functional teams that are responsible for delivering specific projects. You and your team represent your functional group and you will have to be effective at communicating on behalf of your function. The conversations that you have are even more significant. They determine, not only your success but also the success of the organization. Your teams may be involved in multiple initiatives at the same time and conversations may fill a lot of time in your day. The conversations will be important to make good progress and to push the projects into the direction you perceive as the right one. But more importantly, if things go wrong, these conversations will help you keep the team focused in the forward direction and help you recover the project. If you have had the right conversations, others will come out and support you in the time of your need. Also, if you have had the right conversations, others will recognize you for your efforts in the overall success of the organization.

CONVERSATIONS NEED EFFORT

Effective conversations are not about sharing your own thoughts, they are also about listening to others. And not just listen to respond but listen to understand. Every person in the conversation has a role to play and listening to their perspective is as important as sharing yours. Great conversations are not the ones where you win all the arguments, they are the ones where everyone wins. They are about making progress. They are also about staying open to alternatives. Good leaders love to lose an argument as long as it leads to a better solution or more chances to win. You must remember that in a conversation, the objectives are bigger than any individual's beliefs. A conversation also needs to be inclusive, and you must make sure that all the members contribute. A leader must make the extra effort to engage the people and give them the opportunity to voice their thoughts.

Diversity of thoughts is important for success. If you prefer to have conversations with like-minded people, you will end up reinforcing your own thoughts. You should seek out people with diverse backgrounds and thinking. Groups which are afraid of raising concerns and avoid conflict at all cost tend to lose in the long run. Healthy conflict is good, and effective conversations are a way to address the concerns and gain from them. Leaders must make sure that the dissenting voice is heard and that all have a chance to speak up without fear.

HUMAN TO HUMAN CONVERSATIONS

With the advent of technology, there are many new ways to have conversations and some of them do not allow much of the human touch. The media like text message, voice message, chat and email provide additional means of initiating and managing discussions. But nothing can really replace a face to face conversation. For humans, it is important to see the people that we talk to. It is not just about what people say, it is also about how they say it, where they look when they say that and so on, and it is also about the things that they do not say. When we are present to one another, we learn and listen and develop empathy for each other. We all love the joy of being heard and of being understood. Video-based discussions come closest to face to face experience and many orga-nizations are adopting them to improve the quality of the internal conversations. It is your responsibility as a leader to bring human-ness to all the conversations. Here is a story of a global leader who is sharing his experiments and learnings in regard to conversations.

To be kind is more important than to be right. Many times, what people need is not a brilliant mind that speaks but a special heart that listens.

F. Scott Fitzgerald

****

STEPHEN ALEXANDER: FROM A TECHNOLOGIST TO A GLOBAL INFLUENCER

Stephen Alexander (Steve) is the CTO of Ciena, a global leader in networking systems, services and software. Steve always believed that the ability to communicate is the key for the advancement of humanity as a whole. He focused on building skills that could enable the technology to help people communicate better. He holds 21 patents and is a technologist at heart. He has through his work impacted the way people communicate by helping build the internet as we know it, both as a researcher early on by advancing the technology in the field of optical communications, and even more so by moving into the commercial world and creating solutions with Ciena.

He has had various crucial conversations that shaped his own journey and the fate of technology. Through these discussions, he has influenced multiple organizations as well as millions of people around the world. This is the story of his journey from being a technologist to becoming a global influencer.

Early Interest in Communications

Steve was always interested in maths, science and communications. He studied at Georgia Institute of Technology for his bachelor's

119

and master's degrees. He was fascinated by the potential of optical communications and specialized in communications theory as well as microwave systems and optoelectronics.

Coming out of college, he had a number of different opportunities, but to stay true to his personal interest in optical communications, he took a job at MIT Lincoln Laboratory in Lexington, Massachusetts. He started his career working on free-space satellite communication systems using lasers and they were able to produce a number of breakthrough research results and some early prototypes. But the program was set back by the Space Shuttle Challenger disaster in 1986 when all the future flight programs were delayed, and they lost a chance to prove the technology and practical applicability of the research. The team redirected their efforts with funding from Defense Advanced Research Projects Agency and formed a consortium of companies, including MIT, AT&T and DEC, to apply all the research findings to terrestrial fibre communications. They created multiple revolutionary technologies that made the internet faster.

He worked at MIT Lincoln for 12 years and had many 'a-ha' moments during these times. He says, '*As a researcher, you get a great personal reward just from being the first to see or understand something. Some of the technologies that we were pioneering have come to impact the fibre optics industry dramatically. Today we cannot imagine the world without optical communication. The internet would not be the same without it. I feel proud to have been part of the team that has made such a big difference to the world.*'

Steve had the knack of having the right conversations and it helped him in achieving success in various endeavours. It was a prestigious movement for him when within 10 years he was selected as a Senior Staff Member in the laboratory. This was unusual for someone as young as him. As he was good at leading people, simplifying complex problems, and getting the work done. His responsibilities continued to expand and his last position at the laboratory was as an assistant group leader. He achieved continuous career growth in addition to the personal satisfaction of driving unique research results.

As he grew into these leadership roles, he kept getting opportunities to lead important conversations. One of the most important things was the responsibility to explain the emerging technology of optical communications to a variety of different audiences. He had often been giving presentations to the very technical audiences at MIT as well as to sponsoring government agencies who paid for the research. Steve also noticed that not all of the people in the audiences were deeply technical, so he learned to customize his presentations to have effective conversations with them.

In 1994, Steve had one of his important conversations. He asked: How could the technology that he had helped develop, and knew so well, be used to improve communications for more than researchers? He talked with his colleagues and with the local Boston technical community and came across a couple of small start-up companies that were looking to further develop and then commercialize optical communication technology. He accepted a leadership role at a small start-up, which later came to be known as Ciena.

The Journey at Ciena

Steve started pioneering work in the field of Dense Wavelength Division Multiplexed (DWDM) system design. Since DWDM was new to the commercial world and Steve excelled at explaining complex technical topics in a simple way to a variety of audiences, he got many opportunities to represent Ciena to the customers. Steve was also mentored by the head of sales. He had conversations with various sales teams about what the customers really needed to hear and how to link the technology to the business outcomes that customers were looking for. Early on, he became a director in R&D, and was promoted to vice president of transport products, and ultimately named CTO, as Ciena continued to make optical communications more capable and cost effective.

Through the dotcom boom in the mid-1990s into the early 2000s, his team sold and deployed a tremendous amount of optical network capacity that was consumed by the initial roll-out of the internet. Then the market changed as the dotcom boom collapsed and a relatively tough period of his career started. Ciena consolidated all the business units into one that he was leading. He was then both the CTO and the SVP of Products and Technology. To do what was right in this new market environment, he focused his thoughts in two areas: the company interests and the interests of the remaining employees. It was a combination of 'fighting for survival' and 'repositioning the organization' so that it could thrive in what he believed would be the future of the industry. He led quite a few of these conversations at the leadership level about industry evolution and growth of the internet in order to come up with the right strategy for the company. The leadership team concluded that they needed to shrink the business back to the point where they would be able to continue serving their customers as well as invest in technologies necessary for the future. These conversations were tough, but they led to the right decisions.

Steve had to do the restructuring of the R&D side of the company to right-size it for the new marketplace. He reduced the R&D capability to roughly to half of its original size. It was really hard for him to have those conversations with the individuals impacted as he had personally hired a number of people that he ended up having to let go of. He had to shut down a number of sites, discontinue a number of products, and re-engineer the R&D capabilities.

Ciena survived this tough time, though at a substantial personal cost to Steve. Over time as things stabilized, he started to grow the R&D capabilities back along with the company. By the end of

2008, he was able to turn over the product lines to other company leaders and focus specifically on the CTO role for Ciena.

Who Are You Having Your Conversations with?

He believes that his conversations expanded in scope and changed in nature when he joined Ciena. He says, '*I kind of separate the type of conversations that I had as a researcher at MIT from the conversations that I had in the commercial world once I came over to Ciena. However, the quality of the conversations I would argue is critical to success in both the environments.*'

When you are a researcher, you are solving the problems in the field of your study. The conversations Steve had during his pure research days at MIT were around advancing the technology. But when he came to the commercial world at Ciena, he was measured differently. The conversations were all about solving problems that people were willing to pay for. These were about 'How do I solve this problem?' 'Whether it is economically viable?' and 'Whether it is a scalable solution?'

He has also realized that people who are at different levels and roles in the company talk at different levels of understanding and complexity. Steve is a big believer in the fact that if you understand how a thing works well enough, even if it is most complicated, you should be able to explain it in simple terms. If you cannot have a successful conversation about technology with a non-technical person, you cannot hope to be in a leadership role. At the same time, if you are interested in technology and want to know about the latest advancements, you should be able to have a dialogue directly with the research engineers.

You must be able to adjust the conversations depending upon the audience. You may need different dialogues to talk about technology or products with your own executives compared to the dialogues you have with the CXOs of your customers. Steve says,

'It is important to be audience-aware. Be mindful of—Who is your audience? What is it that they want to hear from you and what are they looking forward to when they are meeting with you?'

The Art of Conversations

Steve believes that there are three buckets of conversations that are critical to your success.

Steve says, *'It may sound a little strange, but the first critical conversation is the one you have with yourself. It is about discovering what you are trying to accomplish. Are you doing what you think you should be doing? Are you self-motivated or self-aware, or in other words, true to yourself?'* He believes it is about choosing a field of work that is aligned with your personal goals. It is about your commitment to yourself. Another part of this conversation is about the culture that you are working in. You must ask yourself if the culture of the organization aligns with your own values. It will be difficult for you to contribute if the culture goes against your principles and you have to justify your actions or ignore the actions of those around you all the time.

Steve says, *'The second critical conversation is the one you have when you come into a job. It is with your supervisor or the hiring manager—What are we doing? What problems are we going to solve together and what is my part in it? It is often that you will end up solving a problem that may not be exactly what your manager or you or anyone else initially thought.'*

He shares his own personal experience on this at Lincoln Laboratory. They hired him to build a specific technological component, but it emerged in the discussions that they had not considered another critical aspect of that technology. Steve could not complete his job without the other part and the conversation resulted in expanding his scope.

Steve says, *'The third conversation is the one that you initiate when you become the leader or the manager of a group. This conversation is with folks who are either working for you directly or the team that you are leading for a specific project. The purpose is to make sure that everybody knows what is really going on and what the team is trying to accomplish. I believe this to be critical for success in any kind of complicated project.'*

When he was at MIT, there were different types of people from all over the world, with all sorts of diverse backgrounds, skill sets and interests. This very diverse and eclectic group of people came up with some very interesting ideas. Steve took lead in talking to the individual folks in a way that everybody understood the common objective and that helped move the projects forward. It was his skill with this type of conversations that led to his career growth at MIT.

Listening and Learning

Steve adds that for each of the critical conversations to be successful, you must have the ability to 'listen' and 'understand'. He believes listening is critical to a successful conversation and it is the difference between talking at someone and talking with someone. He believes that one must also listen to the broader conversations that happen at the industry level, for example, publications, conferences and so on. Even if these things are not directed at you, they affect you, so you better be listening.

Steve says that another trick to having great conversations is to keep improving your skills by watching others who communicate well. He says, '*It is about being aware of the folks around you and being observant. If you find it easy to have a conversation with someone, think about why it was easy. Is there something that you can learn from the experience?*'

Handling Difficult Conversations

Steve believes a lot of it has to be about acknowledging upfront that it is going to be a difficult conversation. You must understand

125

that each person in the conversation probably views the difficulty a little bit differently. It is important to let each one of the people talk about their perceptions. Unless there is a deliberate error, a great conversation will convert the difficult situation into a shared tragedy. And then it is a matter of 'how do we work through it?'

It is important to create a 'safety zone' so that people do not hesitate to share the real issues. Sometimes people make a mistake or have a problem that they would rather not talk about in public because it can reflect badly on them. If you create the right environment that is safe, they will confide in you and things will become a whole lot easier. He remembers the first time he had a difficult conversation with a technician about a potential layoff action. Steve set the stage of the discussion such that the technician felt empowered to share his personal problems. They ended up working something out that allowed the technician to manage the problems at home and contribute effectively to the organization.

What Stops People from Having Great Conversations

Steve recalls one time at MIT when there was an incident at the laboratory when an experiment had not gone well because of some equipment damage. It was an expensive mistake and tempers got raised. People suspected a researcher for the failure and exchanged some heated words. Steve recalls personally going and apologizing to that person because it really was an accident and there was nothing malicious in it. There are times when emotions get a hold of you and conversations go wrong. Steve says, '*It can happen with me because I will typically have an emotional reaction to something immediately. I have learned to ignore the emotional component of it and come back to it later. There are many times when I have written an email and then held it back. I come back to it later when the emotion has subsided and decide whether I really want to send it that way, edit it, or just discard it.*'

Then there are times when you listened to the words well but did not watch or observe carefully enough. You may miss having a critical conversation at the right time. For example, sometimes for various reasons people do not want to bring you the bad news, though they may drop the hints in their conversation or in their demeanour. He remembers a couple of instances where if he had paid more attention, he could have avoided some problems. Steve says, *'A person had come in a couple of times to make me aware that there were some slips on the schedule. I thought they could handle it, but it was beyond what they could fix. I did not dig deeper and did not take the pains to understand the details. I missed having conversations at the right time and we could not meet the schedule in one case and had a product problem in the other.'*

It is to be noted that as the organizations become bigger and geographically dispersed, leaders may find it difficult to have all the right conversations. You have to work more diligently at making sure that you find the time to connect and make quality conversations happen.

Another thing that stops people from having a great conversation is a belief that 'they know it all'. Steve says, *'You have to be a little bit willing to be vulnerable because you cannot possibly know everything. If you believe you already know the answer before you go into a conversation, it is not a real conversation. So, you have to go in with the knowledge that the outcome can be different than what you were thinking that things can change, and you can be affected by that change, positively or negatively. And you have got to be open for that exposure.'*

He thinks a lot of time people avoid a discussion for the fear of not having the answer or fear of looking or sounding stupid. They do not want to admit that they may not know the answer.

Then there is also the fear of admitting failure. People always want to look smart; they want to be able to say that they did a good job. They keep on trying to fix things until it is too late. There is a fear of admitting that you need help, that you do not understand or that you are confused. Steve says, '*If, for example, one of my team members came in and admitted that he is confused, we would sit down and talk it out. We would make sure that by the time we were done talking there was no more confusion. Because together we would figure out a way to address the issue, or we will discover what we were doing wrong. That way the team member would have prevented a potential failure and eventually look smarter.*'

What Can Organizations Do to Empower Conversations?

As companies become more diverse geographically, it becomes difficult to build a comfort level between people to facilitate great conversations. Organizations must find ways to make people meet in person. It goes a long way in building the comfort level and cementing the relationship. Once you have met the person, it is easy to continue the conversations later.

The organizations must facilitate video conferencing where meeting in person is difficult. Video helps to facilitate an additional level of human connection compared to talking to someone on the phone. After the connection is established, rapid communication such as texting, messaging and even social media tools like Instagram and so on help a lot in facilitating conversations. For example, people might come across something they think you might be interested in and share that with you to start a conversation. Organizations must provide these tools and help people adopt these tools.

A culture that promotes conversations and empowers dialogue can help you blossom and grow to your potential. An important part is played by the top management of the organization in setting the right culture. Steve believes that the importance of the 'tone at the top' can never be overestimated. The leadership must have better conversations, to the point where just because you disagree does not mean you do not collaborate on getting things done.

How Steve Mentors His Own Team

Steve sets up group conversations with the team on a weekly basis and balances it with one-to-one conversations with each individual, every other week. He prefers to have video calls when face to face meetings are not possible. He makes sure that they have a good team discussion and adjusts conversations based on individual preferences.

He makes sure that his team members are talking to their own teams and regularly mentors the team on conversations. He does some skip-level meetings and reaches out through emails or one-to-one meetings during his travels to make sure his team is doing a good job of having conversations with their team members and other stakeholders in general.

What Steve Says for Your Next Promotion

Knowing your audience and customizing your conversations accordingly is very important. At the executive level, you have to be able to communicate differently because you are talking to people who are experts in either management, finance, human relations, legal, sales, marketing and so on. You should be able to make a connection with these people and communicate effectively.

While having difficult conversations, it is good to practice the conversation with a colleague or a mentor or someone else. You should be able to view the points and the potential counterpoints and go back and forth to make sure you got it right. It can help you overcome the fears that hold you back from an open and honest conversation.

It pays to build a rapport at a personal level with the people you want to have conversations with. If you can talk about common interests, it will become more than a pure business dialogue. You must be respectful of other's privacy but having some common ground helps in creating a platform for great conversations, it could be a common sports team that you both admire, or a hobby you both have.

Steve says that the advancement of the ranks often leads to dealing with more and more ambiguity. The ability to use conversations to turn ambiguity into understanding and then using the understanding to solve larger problems at work becomes extremely important. Your world view expands as you go higher up in the organization. Understanding the various roles within

Message for Millennials

Steve thinks that a lot of people are held back by fear or uncertainty about spoiling their impression on the manager. He encourages them to get to know the manager, a little bit on a personal level. Steve encourages youngsters to have one-on-one meetings with their managers to build the bond. He says that the millennials must develop the habit of having more one-on-one conversations in addition to the social media conversations they have.

the organization as well as the role of your organization in the greater context of the competitive marketplace becomes important. It is about having an awareness of the market and business. You should be able to use conversations within the company as well as outside to build that awareness. You should also be able to represent the activities of your company in conversations you have within the industry.

Steve believes that the right conversations will make the path forward much smoother and fulfilling.

****

130

ALL CONVERSATIONS ARE NOT GREAT

You all have conversations at work and beyond, and you also spend a lot of time thinking about those conversations. Conversations are a critical part of your work life; they lead to various decisions and actions that propel your organizations and your careers forward. Though a lot of discussions take place, I still hear leaders complaining about miscommunication and misunderstanding. There must be something missing in those discussions. Even when lot of conversations are cordial, they do not create the impact they should. You must strive to have meaningful and productive conversations. But before we talk about how to go about creating meaning for all the people involved in a conversation, let us try and understand what can stop you from having great conversations.

You Are Not Aware

You do not notice the signs of a conversation going wrong, because you are too absorbed in your own idea. All you want to do is make sure that you are able to communicate your thoughts. You ignore the signs of disinterest in the other people and push on. Or, you believe that the idea you are communicating is quite simple to understand and leave no space for questions or clarifications. Remember that if it is a monologue, it is not a conversation.

You Do Not Spend Time to Know People

You go into to the meeting not knowing the people you are talking to. You do not spend time trying to build on a common interest. You do not engage to understand their objectives from the conversation. It may seem that you do not speak the same language as the other person in the room, making the dialogue ineffective.

You Do Not Spend Time to Prepare

Preparation is the key to a successful conversation. But if you did not have time to prepare, you may be utilizing the time over trivial things. Let us say you had only 15 minutes with the executive leader to share an idea that will take an hour for you to discuss properly. Would you be successful if you go in anyway and start explaining the idea and the meeting ends before you got to the interesting piece of the discussion?

You Do Not Listen

You have too much to say and you do not want to lose your chance to say it all. Or you hear but do not listen. In other words, you understand only to the extent it aligns with your own beliefs. You pick up the pieces of the conversation that work for you and ignore the rest. You brush aside concerns or delay the answers to them to a later date. People can notice and feel when you are there to tell them stuff versus when you want a genuine discussion.

I Am Right

You start the conversation with the premise that you already know the answer, that you know it all. You believe that others are ignorant. You will not listen at all or at the very best, listen to respond. You will provide your rebuttal for every claim or counterclaim, sending a clear message that 'It is my way or the highway' and that it is futile to raise any concerns.

You Assume

You assume that everyone understands you very well and that everyone is quite clear. When they do not ask questions, does that mean they understand? If you do not ask for confirmatory questions or seek their suggestions, they may keep their doubts in their own head and never really appreciate what you said.

Or you assume that they do not want to understand, or they do not consider what you are saying as important, so you just want the experience to end for the sake of all involved and just rush through your points.

Long Way to Success

Sometimes one conversation does not lead to any conclusion and neither does it seem like you are making any headway. You try again and do not make much progress. If you do not see any progress you will not continue to invest your energy into it. For example, if the matters that you are discussing are about a relatively bigger change, others may resist your ideas and seek not to cooperate. The path to the success is longer in such cases and you may give up too soon.

WHAT ARE GREAT CONVERSATIONS MADE OF?

Conversations are about people. People want to partner, they want to contribute, they have ideas that they want to discuss and you need to work together to achieve success. All this starts with a conversation and when people leave the discussion; they will remember how you made them feel. This feeling will propel them to the next action. So great conversations make sure that the people leave with right feelings.

Here are a few recommendations to make your conversations powerful.

Intention

Every important business conversation will lead to some change. While the change can be good or bad in the long run, it may be disturbing in the short run. The moment people sense some disturbance, they may resist it and you may lose them from the conversation. You should make it clear in the beginning that your intentions are to be of help in some way. That the conversation is not about making them uncomfortable but better prepared for success in future. That what you have to offer, compliments their own efforts and that you are on the same side of the table, not opposite. If you convey your intentions, the conversation will become more open and easier.

Attention and Understanding

Pay attention to others, listen to understand, ask questions, be inquisitive, be genuine in your efforts to understand their points. Like I said before, humans perform best when they feel included and own a piece of the action. Give importance to others and seek their support, let them know that they matter and what they say is important to you. They will be happy to have a conversation with you and will walk away with a feeling of their own significance in the scheme of things. Any agreements you achieve will be honoured.

Trust

You must make effort to build trust with the other people, even before the conversations. If you know the person from before, it becomes easier. Familiarity begets trust, so you must find some common ground to start with, it could be simple stuff, such as, you like same type of food or follow the same game or like a recent piece of news. Make sure you build some familiarity to begin with and then use every additional opportunity to build on that trust.

Space and Time

Make space in your discussions for others to participate. Give them time to think on what you said and help them reflect upon the implications by seeking their own understanding of what you said. Similarly, when you are listening to others, repeat what you understood, make sure you get the grasp of what is said, ask questions and seek time to evaluate things for yourself before you commit. The space and time will allow people to consider the options and then they can come up with new ideas that can augment the conversations.

Manage Emotions

It is not possible to have a balanced conversation when you are run over by emotions. Some comments can put you off guard and you may lose the opportunity to have a great conversation. The truth is that not every time things turn out to be what we seek. The shock of unfavourable news can overwhelm us or others in the discussions and things can easily take a negative turn. You must be aware of your emotions and know when to take a break. You must not let your emotions get the better of you. Similarly, when someone else in running high on emotions, you must make an effort to understand and allow them time to collect themselves.

Ask Open-ended Questions

The best way to involve others into a conversation is to ask them open-ended questions. Do not let them limit their responses to 'yes I agree'. Seek opinions, thoughts, concerns, doubts or raise your own. Great conversations are not the ones that end early or end without any conflict, they are the ones that help you get more clarity and help create a path forward. You must not assume to know the answer and should always take up the role of a seeker.

TRANSFORM YOUR MINDSET

Your awareness will help you anchor the right thoughts in your mind.

FIXED MINDSET	GROWTH MINDSET
They do not know how to talk.	People are different, let me understand what she means.
I am not happy with what you have been doing.	How can I help you to do this better?
You are not saying it in the right way.	How can I ask more questions to understand?
I just cannot tolerate him.	I am here to co-create a better place.
Can you just come straight to the point?	What is the most important thing here?

GREAT CONVERSATIONS: IN ACTION

The following few questions will help you to reflect on conversations. I suggest you learn from your reflections and continue to dig deeper.

- Who can provide you feedback on your skills at conversations? Seek their time to get specific feedback about one or two conversations that they were also a part of.

- How good are you at listening? Do you listen to respond or listen to understand?

- Is your style of conversation affected by the level of the person you talk to? Do you feel more in control if you are the most senior person in the conversation? How can you change the experience of people who are junior to you?

- How can you voice your opinion without being offensive?

- Remember the last five important conversations that you recently had.

> Rate your experience on a scale of 1–10.

> Which conversation went the best? Please note down the factors that made it great.

- Your comfort level with the subject
- Your comfort level with the people
- Others

> If you had to repeat this conversation again, would you be able to improve your experience? If so, how?

> Which conversation went the worst? Please note down the factors that made it bad.

- You did not get time to prepare
- You were not engaged
- Emotions ran high
- Others

> If you had to repeat the worst conversation again, what will you do differently?

- What do you think you need to learn for becoming better at conversations?

- Which of your strengths can help you to have great conversations?

Leadership is about magnetic communication.
Leaders have a way of communicating that draws
people toward the vision and the horizon.

Doug Firebaugh

8

CREATING VISIBILITY AND PERSONAL BRANDING

❝ ❞

Your personal brand is what people say about you when you are not in the room—remember that. And more importantly, let's discover why!

CHRIS DUCKER

Well sometimes it happens that despite all your efforts, hard work, passion and even results that help the organization move forwards, you stay stuck, while others may keep on growing. That makes you wonder what is wrong with you. You believe that you

- Are hardworking and never skip a deadline

- Have great ideas and believe strongly in them

- Drive results, through commitments and teamwork

You believe you are an important pillar of the organization and have been contributing a lot but somehow the organization is not rewarding you for that. If it happens that you are skipped more than once, you might start believing that there is a conspiracy against you and that someone is deliberately holding you back.

You may get some feedback highlighting your areas of development. Now you might think that they are just excuses as you already have those qualities and sometimes even more than what is needed. Then what is the issue?

THE ISSUE IS QUITE SIMPLE

It is about being noticed for those qualities. Perception is reality. If you are not seen demonstrating these qualities and no one talks about you in relation to these qualities, leaders may carry a perception that you do not have them.

You must also make sure that you get noticed in the right way. Blowing your own trumpet may not be the right way, sometimes that is taken as arrogance or some sort of superiority complex. You need to work on creating visibility for yourself and there are many ways that you can achieve it, without being wrong. Make sure that you align yourself better with your organization's success. Think about who has great visibility and reflect on what they do differently. Consider the following aspects, they may provide few insights.

Are You a Loner or a Leader?

When you work on projects that are important to the organization, do you bear in mind that you should not be pushing your own ideas on everyone else? You may have the best idea and do not realize the need to make sure that ideas of other people are heard and evaluated. Do you encourage others to come up with their ideas? Are you open to adapt and accept better aspects from ideas of other people? Do you help the organization find the right path by helping the team evaluate everything objectively and comprehensively? Do you keep the best interests of the organization in your mind and take others along? In a team project, one cannot just win alone; the whole team wins. If you are perceived as a loner, it may go against you.

Are You Being Helpful?

Once the course of action is decided, do you make sure that you do your part and help others complete their part as well? Do you keep the ball rolling or assume that as long as you have done your part you are good? The person who takes initiative to support other team members is always appreciated and noticed. Do not think that this is a waste of time, this thought process may hold you back. If the project gets stuck and you knew about it, do you get into the mode, 'I told you so' or get into a problem-solving mode? Helping chart a course that will take the team on the path to a victory may be the right approach.

Are You Leveraging All Your Strengths?

Do you offer access to additional resources to make things easier for the team? Your resourcefulness will be appreciated, and people will reach out to you for your support. If more people consider you helpful, more people will talk about you and sooner or later you will get noticed.

Organizations care for people who care for the organization; do you help discover easier ways to do things, help save time, effort and cost for the organization? Do you listen to leaders and understand the challenges they are trying to solve? Make every effort to address some of the challenges in your projects or your day-to-day work. Make sure that you get the message back into your organization in case your project is able to achieve some of these objectives.

BUT IS VISIBILITY ENOUGH?

You must also make sure that you stand for something. In other words, you must have your own brand. When do people remember you? When they are facing a certain type of problem? Or when they need some help with a specific work? Or when they are stuck and looking for guidance? What do you stand for? When they look at you, what is the first word that comes to their mind?

Brand in a way is what people associate you with. You must cultivate the right brand that aligns with your career goals. If you want to build a career in marketing, your brand image should be of a person who has a polished personality and who can deliver messages powerfully and effectively, who can say more with less, who is great at presentations, who can paint a vision in a few pictures, who can simplify the complex and make it all easy to understand.

Take a moment to think about your current brand image, you may seek feedback to learn what people perceive about you. Then think of what you would want it to be. Reflect upon the gaps. This will help you understand what you might need to do. Remember that your brand helps you to differentiate yourself from the others.

One must get noticed in the right way and should be noticed for the right things. And it is never too early to start building that space for yourself. Let us read the story of a leader who had a knack of differentiating himself and learn from it.

****

MALUR NARAYAN: MAKING DREAMS COME TRUE

A focus on 'what can be' instead of 'what is' and a refusal to let limitations stop him has enabled Malur, a Vice President at TCS, USA to successfully reinvent himself throughout his career. He has had more than two decades of experience in IT and Telecom industry spread equally between North America and Asia. He has taken up new challenges and posted one success after another. He has built a strong personal brand by pioneering new ways of working and creating new avenues of business. He has succeeded against all odds in a broad range of senior management roles ranging from sales, business development, product management, marketing, and product development. He is known for his positive attitude and is an eminent speaker on International business at various international forums and today his brand extends across continents and industries. Let us peep into a few pages of his career.

Humble Beginnings and Big Dreams

Malur did most of his early education in India. His family moved every few years to a different city, which gave him the skills to adapt to new environment and make new friends. He started with Bachelor of Science at National College in Bangalore, but transitioned a year later to computer engineering, which at the time, was a new and upcoming field. In 1989, he graduated first in the University and won a gold medal for his accomplishments. He wanted to go overseas to pursue his dreams. He knew that his family would not be able to afford to send him abroad, so he had to figure out a lot of things on his own, especially finances. He won several scholarships for financing his travel as well as education. He challenged the constraints and set the stage for a bright future.

Setting New Standards

He pursued a master's degree in technology from the University of Western Ontario in Canada. Two emerging fields—machine learning and AI, seemed the most intriguing to him—and he decided to specialize in these. Typically, a master's degree, takes up to two years to complete the coursework, which is spread over three or four semesters. Malur chose the difficult path, '*I decided to take all the coursework in the first semester itself. Which was unheard of. I figured I will do all the coursework first and get it out of the way. Then I can just spend the rest of my time doing the research.*'

After his master's degree, he accepted a job offer from Bell Northern Research (BNR), later known as Nortel. BNR was an R&D unit. He moved to Ottawa to join BNR.

The First Real Job: Thinking Differently

The first task he was assigned was quite unlike what he had done before. He was hired into BNR as a technical writer and not as a software engineer. BNR had a custom digital telecom software that lacked product documentation and it was nearly impossible to make any changes to it without disrupting the code. He was hired as a part of a team to go through all the code and write a system description about it. He took advantage of his software development background and wrote a software program that extracted the required information. It sped up the whole process and became a big hit with his leaders. He says, '*Suddenly instead of having to write about everything we had a quick visual way of figuring out how it all works.*' Based on the number of people who used this software, he generated an internal revenue of about two million dollars. That was the first big success for him in his career.

He spent the first six years working under the same organization building and developing multiple releases of the software and building it into a large team of about 20 people. Malur had differentiated himself as a person who had the ability to find the right thing to do and make it a success. He became the team leader and then fast-tracked to a manager within three years of joining BNR.

The director of his organization at BNR, Steve Malcolm, took notice of Malur's work. He was impressed by the way Malur built this software tool and the revenue it was generating and how much interest it had generated within the organization. Steve saw a lot of potential in Malur, and he started to coach him one-on-one. Malur recalls, Steve telling him, '*You can do great things, but unless you tell others, you would not be noticed.*' That is when the earliest thoughts about building a personal brand started forming. Back then he did not call it by that name. Steve became one of the first role models that Malur looked up to. Steve sponsored an Executive MBA for Malur at the University of Ottawa.

A strong people culture at BNR helped Malur inculcate human values like care and empathy in his personal brand.

Building the Career: Continuing to Create the Brand

After completing the MBA, he took up a product management role. He was managing a critical portfolio of products for Nortel. Malur says, '*My direct boss Perry Mangione was also very instrumental in developing my early managerial skill set. I think all the managers that I had, were very forthcoming, extremely supportive and always encouraged dialogue, free and out of the box thinking. It had a fundamental influence on me and how I dealt with my own teams.*'

He started work on a product called Broadband STP. It was a new technology that was instrumental in bridging the old telecom world with the new Internet Protocol world. Malur again got into deep waters with it and got a chance to launch this in various markets around the globe. Through these new initiatives, he got exposure to international markets and to launching a new product in new market spaces. People now recognized him for his technical expertise and as well as business acumen.

Learning from the Other Side of the Table

In 1999, he took a year-long sabbatical and joined Bell Canada International (BCI), which was a sister company of Nortel. BCI used to own various telecom operators globally in Latin America, Europe, Korea and even in India, they had a partnership with the Tata Group. He joined as a consultant and worked with the local operators in Venezuela and Brazil. That whole business was going through transformation because of deregulation (a process through which private businesses and foreign telecom operators were allowed into telecom infrastructure business).

There he learned a lot about the operator side while evaluating various technologies for wireless networks. It was an interesting experience that helped him gain a much broader perspective of the business and add additional experience of diverse geographical locations. Very few people take such career risks and he made this transition successfully. This helped strengthen his brand within Nortel.

Coming Back and Making the Most of It

When he came back after the sabbatical in 2000, Nortel was doing really well. Its stock had gone up, and it was worth over 250 billion at one point, even bigger than Microsoft. He had a lot of opportunities for different jobs. He got selected to be a director of Bell Canada within Nortel and had another offer in the USA with another company, but he chose a two-year assignment based in Singapore to lead the Southeast Asia wireless business under the leadership of Jean-Luc Jezouin. Jean-Luc was a charming and brilliant individual, very analytical. Malur worked closely with him and learned a lot on positioning solutions and building customer relationships.

This was another interesting time in his life, he had transitioned from product development or software development to product management, product marketing and now he was doing sales and sales support out in the field. He was responsible for driving new revenue for Nortel and working with all the local operators in Southeast Asia.

In early 2000s, India was also going through a big change in deregulation, so India became a big piece of his business. They won a large number of deals and that business grew a lot. He was recognized for the success. Over time, he built a strong team in Singapore and in other parts of Southeast Asia including India. Based on his success in Asia, in 2004 he was offered a role in India to establish the wireless unit, and he moved to Mumbai to take it up under the leadership of Michael Murphy, Ashoka Valia and later Anthony Mclachlan.

Forging Ahead through Tough Times: What Helped Was His Visibility and Brand

For next four–five years, Nortel went through a rough time because of various issues including a financial scandal and the financial crisis in 2007. That took an ugly turn by 2008. Though Asia was doing well, Nortel went through bankruptcy in 2009.

Malur was looking for his next big break, seeking opportunity to get into the executive team, but he was facing some challenges, as the company was not doing too well. Malur decided to try something else and leveraging his network he reached out to Steve Slattery, who was the head of the global enterprise business. Malur was always ready to step out of his comfort zone to create a bigger impact. Steve wanted him to take up product management for enterprise business in Asia. It was a completely new role for him, a new product line, new market, new way of doing business and totally new people. So, in 2006, he took a job with the enterprises division and got to explore a very different side of the business.

He gives a lot of credit to Nortel for letting him try new things from time to time. What always came in handy was the brand image that Malur had built over the years. He had proven that he could take up new things and make them work. He had business experience and a proven track record, so the lack of technical knowledge of the enterprise portfolio did not become a hurdle. He moved from an area of strength, where he knew technology and people to an area full of unknowns. By end of two years, he had built a new set of capabilities, relationships and was at home in his new environment.

They built that business over time and it was doing well. But when bankruptcy discussions came on and Nortel needed more help with potential partners, Malur decided to do one year of business alliances work to help build a stronger partner network for the company. He had built great relationships with companies like TCS and Wipro and decided to leverage these to help Nortel.

He remembers a defining moment that happened in 2007. Nortel was in the process of signing a deal with Tata group companies. There was a meeting organized between Ratan Tata, Chairman of Tata Group, and Mike Z, Nortel CEO in New York. Since Malur was the one who was working on the deal, he joined his CEO for this critical meeting. That is when he met Chandra (Natarajan Chandrasekaran) who later became the chairman of the Tata group. They were sitting next to each other and hit it off well. Malur kept in touch with Chandra when he came back to India. Once when TCS was bidding on a Nortel project and they were facing challenges. Chandra called him to seek help. Malur facilitated a meeting between TCS and Nortel's executives and that really impressed Chandra.

Malur always left great impressions on people that he worked with. He has been successful in building a great image even through troublesome times in Nortel. When Nortel was going through the bankruptcy proceedings, Chandra offered him a role in TCS. Malur decided to join.

Building a Brand beyond Telecom

Malur chose to work in the headquarters of TCS. He worked for Telecom Sector under Chandra and helped to build that business. It was not a smooth ride; he remembers instances when despite all the efforts and his connections he lost a large deal after being close to winning it. Malur says *'Things do happen for various reasons. Some beyond your control. That time you suffer as you have failed to contribute significantly compared to others. Results affect you too. You do not get the credit and rightly so.'* But a proven track record and a strong brand helped Malur to reduce the impact of such instances. Over time Malur had created a space for himself in the IT world.

In 2012, Chandra asked Malur to take over the Tata group relationship, which was another defining point in his career. TCS was working on a project called 'Customer Centricity' which was basically taking all the customer data of various Tata Group companies and then trying to put together an analytics-based system like the Big Data. This helped him build relationships with the senior leaders in the Tata Group and enhance his brand within TCS as well as within the Tata Group.

Moving to USA and into the Current Role

In 2015, Malur decided to move to USA and he picked up another challenge. He had a strong Telecom background, so he took charge of driving new business with semiconductor and networking companies in the USA. He became vice president, Technology Business Group. Malur now leads the technology vertical in TCS in North America and handles the business with semiconductor companies, networking companies, devices companies like Cisco, AMD, Intel and so on.

Building Brand, the Right Way

Malur says, *'If you get early success and you rise through the ranks quickly and become a leader, you start realizing that you have a tough competition. That you need to be seen and noticed by many others in the organization other than your manager and his manager. Without the right network that knows your value you may end up being stagnant.'*

He was one of the first persons on LinkedIn and advocates the use of social networking tools. In the days before such tools, he however, had to build the network by physically meeting people or by talking to them on phone.

Throughout his career, Malur got opportunities to work in multiple profiles and to explore quite a few aspects of the business.

Almost, all of those roles were offered to him by someone from his network. There is a saying, 'Beyond a point in your career, what really matters is who knows that you know.' He worked hard to build relationships within and outside the organization. The fact that he produced results, got him the chance to do more and every time he got new opportunities, he worked harder to make sure that he exceeded expectations. Today people can vouch for his ability to build strong relationships and leave a lasting impression.

Malur says, '*I suggest that the best time of building right connections is when you do not need something from the person you are trying to build a connection with. When nothing is at stake. Then you can meet as equals and explore possibilities. If you both see value in each other, make the effort to stay connected. That way when you call that person to ask for something, you will not be seen coming out of nowhere.*'

The What and How of Personal Brand

Malur believes that your personal branding is what you call your reputation. It is critical in any role. At the end of the day, any role that has a requirement to interact with a lot of people requires you to build some personal reputation. And for that to happen, you need to have a few things:

- *Credibility:* You need to establish credibility whenever you go into a new role or whenever you are dealing with a new bunch of people. They may have heard certain things from other people about you. But you must establish credibility in the first few months of that interaction.

- *Say/Do ratio:* People need to be able to trust you. You need to be able to be seen like somebody who does things that they say they will.

- *Easy to approach:* If you are easy to approach, people will come to you.

How Do You Know if You Are Making Progress on Building Your Brand?

The brand is a cumulative set of people's perceptions and you will see that happening over time. You must build great expertise in whatever you do and become knowledgeable about your subject and then you must spread that knowledge by sharing it. There is also something called executive presence which comes down to being confident and being able to deliver a message with authority. When you say something, you must mean it. It is a slow process, suddenly people will not start recognizing you. You have to build on your trust, credibility and approachability.

He says, '*If you become more approachable and take more genuine interest in other people's issues, things will start to change. When more people start approaching you, you will know that you are making progress.*'

Where Can People Go Wrong with Brand Building?

- *Shortcuts:* The first thing is a lot of people like to take shortcuts. Personal brand development takes a lot longer. One must continuously work on it, and you know there are a lot of books that you can read, a lot of videos you can watch in terms of personal growth and building personality. Ninety per cent of building a personal brand also has a lot to do with your own personality. You must become more approachable and start offering help and not always think about taking more.

- *Love for titles:* Second, people do not focus on the process or goal but focus on the title. You must focus more on where you want to get to. Create goals and think about how you bridge the gaps.

- *Trying too hard:* Third, when you try to make an impression, sometimes it can come across as too aggressive. Building a brand starts with building relationships, whether it is via email or in person on phone, always be humble and listen to others.

What Can Organizations Do to Support Brand Building?

- The biggest thing that organizations can do is to create more opportunities for people to network in person as much as possible. It can be a simple thing like everybody in the company meets up on a regular basis in an environment where people can socialize and at the same time seek guidance.

- Enable an environment where they can interact one-on-one.

- Enable a formal structure which has mentors and mentees paired on a regular basis. Create a holistic selection process of mentors and mentees.

How Does He Mentor His Own Team

- Malur talks to his team regularly. He makes sure to create trusting relationship with his team.

- He shares his perspective on to building networks, relationships and personal brand.

- He gives honest feedback. He tells what he feels is positive and what he feels they can improve, and shares where he sees the gaps. He also tells them that everything he says is not gospel and that they need to also talk to other people and get their feedback.

What Malur Says about Your Next Promotion

Malur has had a rich career filled with changes and diverse experiences, he has come out as a winner through tough times. He shares his wisdom with all those who seek to excel.

He says that there can be times in one's life when one is feeling lost. Maybe other people are getting the promotion instead of you. Or you are feeling like your career is in a stalemate. And people tell you a lot of things such as 'you did not get that job because you do not have executive presence,' or 'you did not meet a particular criterion' and so on. You must take all the feedback in perspective, but you must realize that people hire people that they are familiar and are comfortable with. If you are seeking a promotion, you cannot start building the relationship the day the job is advertised. You must start a couple of years before. Find out a way to get some assignments, learn the missing skills and be seen as already doing the role. If people see you doing the job and being passionate about it, then when the job comes up, it becomes an easy sell.

'Today's environment is fast-changing. But people always think that things are going to be stationary, that maybe their leader will still be around three years from now and that maybe that role will not open up for another few years. But people leave the company, organizations restructure, companies get merged, acquired and so on. Especially in this day and age, changes are more rapid. You look for the job that you really want and build your brand accordingly.'

He says *'Forget about titles. You will not get too far if you get hung up on titles. Titles mean nothing and these days they are*

Message for Millennials

It is easy for millennials to switch attention from one task to another. Malur advises youngsters to do the following:

- Try different things but at the same time give each thing a little more time.

- Take about as many risks as possible because you have the least amount to lose when you are young.

- You can try different things and figure out what is your calling, what you enjoy doing.

- It is good to have a lot of enthusiasm, but it is also about how much you are willing to learn too. Learn as much as you can.

dime a dozen, anybody can be a chief of whatever. So, what you really need to worry about is what function or what role do you want to perform.'

You need to figure out what is your calling and what is it that you enjoy doing. Because if you enjoy doing it, you will do it really well and you will succeed. So do not focus on the title, focus on the function. Identify a person in that role and look at that person's job. If you have a role model or if you have somebody that you think is doing a great job, then identify what is the gap between where you are and where you want to be. Whether it is in terms of skill sets, experience, network, systems or knowledge, you can bridge that gap. Anybody can do anything but how well you can do it depends on how passionate you are about it.

Malur feels that brand building is not a flash in the pan, it is integral to your growth and an ongoing journey.

****

WHAT STOPS PEOPLE FROM BUILDING A STRONG BRAND

There are two big buckets of reasons, the first one around beliefs and the second one around knowledge.

Belief that Your Work Speaks for Itself

As explained in the first two chapters of the book, early in your career, especially when you are contributing dependently or independently, the main value that you deliver is your work. The quantity and quality of the work matter a lot and help you differentiate yourself. The faster you learn the task the better it is, the better quality you deliver the more you are appreciated. This approach sticks with you and you tend to depend on your work to speak for you.

Belief that Getting Noticed Can Be Bad

You believe that showcasing your work is bragging and you shy away from highlighting your achievements. This will stop you from getting additional responsibilities and your scope may not grow. But your growth depends on expanding your scope, the more you handle, the bigger your impact. The bigger your impact the more you get noticed. But you need to be noticed first to get the additional scope. As long as you try to stay low, you will not get noticed and may not get additional scope and this becomes a vicious cycle that prevents you from using your full potential.

Belief that It Is Not Your Job

You believe that it is your manager's job to notice all the work that you do and to see the potential in you. That if you are not getting any rewards, it is your manager's fault and not yours. This may well be true again for the first two stages of the career. As you grow up and pick bigger roles, the number of stakeholders grow and your visibility needs to extend beyond your manager.

Lack of Knowledge to Build the Brand

The last part that holds you back is the fact that you do not know how to go about it. You do not know what the best brand statement would be for yourself. You have been focused on completing projects and assignments and have not had the time to sharpen your skills or hone your strengths.

You are good at quite a few things but have not branded yourself as best at any one thing. In other words, you may be the best at something, but no one knows about it and you do not know how to let others know about it. You never got the opportunity to showcase yourself and do not know what you should do to get a chance.

YOU DO NOT NEED TO BE A PRO TO BUILD YOUR BRAND

All you need to do is, take a few actions. But each will take some additional work. Creating a brand takes a conscious effort. Consider the following few to start with.

Create Time

The first thing you need is time and if you are always busy firefighting, you may not be able to spare the time for branding. You may benefit by effective delegation and effective time management.

Choose Your Brand

Once you have created time, take the opportunity to review your strengths and select those that you want to be known for. Understand the priorities for your leader and pick up additional things that you can do to make your leader successful. Make sure that the tasks you pick up are aligned with the brand you want to create. Your leader will recognize your efforts and start looking for you every time a similar task comes up.

Exhibit the Values You Stand For

Set examples through your day-to-day conduct. For example, if you believe in respecting others, show it by listening to their opinions, being curious about their thoughts and by helping them develop on their ideas. Become a beacon of good values and you will get noticed for the same.

Seek Multidimensional Projects

These projects will help you in two ways: first, you will get the understanding of the big picture, and second, you be representing your whole function to other departments. Share ideas and help develop new ones. If you are able to contribute to the success of such projects, you will leave a positive impression on multiple stakeholders, and you will position yourself as a 'go to' person for your function.

If your project is important, and brings benefits to the organization, make sure that your leader knows about the project and the benefits. Remember to share credit with your team.

Develop Others

Take active interest in developing others. There will be many people in the organization, your juniors and your peers who can benefit from your wisdom, experience, knowledge, connections and so on. Always be open to help. Helping more people become successful with your power and ability will make the ripples of it felt throughout the organization. People will look up to you and the management will know. A positive side-effect of this is that your own network starts growing and your ability to make things happen start growing even more.

Be a Thought Leader

Your organization needs a lot of collateral to market and position itself in the industry. Contribute white papers, blogs and so on and seek opportunities to represent your organization at industry events. This will help establish your brand outside as well.

TRANSFORM YOUR MINDSET

Branding is about doing the right things and leaving right impressions. A growth mindset will help you achieve that.

FIXED MINDSET	GROWTH MINDSET
My work will speak for me.	How is my work helping others? How can I make them aware of it?
People are too busy to notice me.	How can I make a difference to people?
I am good at everything.	How can I differentiate myself?

FIXED MINDSET	GROWTH MINDSET
I do not know what brand I need to create.	Who can I take help from?
I do not know what brand I have right now.	How can I take feedback to understand my current brand?

PERSONAL BRANDING: IN ACTION

The following few questions will help you to reflect on branding.

- What are the three values that define you?
- What are your top three strengths?
- How do you showcase those values and strengths at work?
- Who can give you feedback on your brand?
- If you cannot tell people your job title, how will you introduce yourself?
- Write four lines of your brand story people should know? In other words, if you have to create an elevator pitch for yourself, what would it be?
- Who can help you create the right brand?
- How do you exhibit your brand by the way you appear? (i.e., dress and manners etc.)
- Do you think people are aware of your brand?
- What can you do so that people acknowledge that brand?
- What opportunities you need to showcase yourself?

The keys to brand success are self-definition, transparency, authenticity and accountability.

Simon Mainwaring

9

CONTINUING LEARNING AND DEVELOPMENT

❝ ❞

The problem with strengths that have led to success is a result of success itself. It is difficult to abandon what has worked, even when circumstances change, and it may be nearly impossible to give up old patterns if no new skills have been developed to replace the old ones.

EXCERPTS FROM 'DIM SUM LEADERSHIP' BY JOHN NG.

Success is your friend, it gets you what you want, recognition, wealth, respect and many such things. But it can also be your enemy. Success can bring with itself arrogance, overconfidence and self-importance. Each success takes you on to a higher plateau, but if you start believing that you have learned all you had to, then you may not progress beyond the current plateau. You must always be learning and growing. Even purest water may start stinking if it stays stagnant for long.

BEEN THERE, DONE THAT

You have been successful so far, that is the reason you are here. You have learned a lot and have achieved wonders. Many may have been reaching out to you to seek your guidance. This may make you feel important and confident. You have seen challenges and overcome them, you have created new formulae for success, and you feel great.

You might want to continue to apply the same formulae forever. But you may find that the path ahead does not seem to be clear and that your next move still seems far. What you choose to do next is important, whether

- You say to yourself, 'been there, done that' and 'who knows better than me' and keep pushing.

- You realize that it may be time to learn something new, that you may need to change to succeed. That there is something different about the next segment of the career path.

It is indeed difficult to teach successful people new things, unless they fail first.

WOULD YOU WANT TO FAIL?

I know you will say 'No, why should I?' I agree, not knowingly and definitely not deliberately. But you may be setting yourself up to fail, if you stop learning. You are in a VUCA world where changes happen, on a daily basis if not faster. Just to give you a small indication, 5–7 TED talks are published per week, meaning about 300+ a year. Each of the TED talk shares an idea or a story from which we can learn.[1] And this is besides the other knowledge sharing platforms such as 'Singularity University', the Podcasts, YouTube Channels and so on. The fact is that a lot of knowledge is being generated each day and as we move forwards, the rate of generation of this knowledge is going to increase. You must not wait to fail before you realize that you are out of touch. By then it will be too late.

HOW MUCH TIME YOU DEVOTE TO LEARNING?

Yes, the question is how many hours? Per week? And what may be the right percentage of time to be spent on learning?

Medium.com published an article, 'Bill Gates, Warren Buffet and Oprah; All Use The 5-Hour Rule'.[2] It says that successful leaders spend at least five hours per week on learning, deliberately. This is apart from what they learn on the job by interacting with other smart people. So, what do they do with this time? The article adds further that the leaders spend time reading, reflecting and experimenting. Each of these contribute to learning.

How about you? How much time do you devote to learning?

IT IS NEVER TOO LATE TO LEARN

Ideally, one must never stop learning, but you must know that there is no age limit for learning and that there is no organizational title that is big enough to exclude learning. If you find yourself stuck at a plateau despite all the great things you have done, you must realize that it is time to get back to learning. I guess if you are reading this book, you are seeking knowledge to achieve your best. I must congratulate you on your initiative and I believe the next level of success is not very far from you. This chapter is to let you know that you are on the right track and you must continue to learn more about your own subject matter as well as learn more about the relevant aspects of leadership.

The greatest leaders always consider themselves as students and they never stop learning.

WHAT CAN LEARNING DO FOR YOU?

The ability to learn is the most important quality a leader can have.

Sheryl Sandberg

I would like to mention three top benefits.

- *It keeps you humble:* Every time you learn something new, it makes you realize that there may be better ways of doing things compared to what you knew. That keeps you from becoming overconfident, know-all type of a personality.

- *It keeps you open:* As you learn, you become open to ideas, open to relooking at your thoughts, open to redefining the problems and open to discovery. These attributes encourage free thinking in your team. The impact is manifold, your whole team will become creative. Creativity will lead to innovation and so on.

- *It makes you share:* When you learn, you gain knowledge that others share. As you apply that knowledge and gain insights from it, you like to spread that knowledge. When you share the knowledge, your reputation builds up. People start looking up to you, they benefit from a discussion with you, they seek you out, you build a strong brand for yourself. This brand will soon extend beyond your function, your organization and your industry.

These benefits are beyond the advantages of applying the new knowledge in your day to work and life.

WHEN DO YOU FIND THE TIME TO LEARN?

You make your plans and then life happens. You get busy and the easiest thing to ignore is your need to learn. Your need to learn does not impact your today, you still know how to do things and you can get by without learning. You push the learning to tomorrow. And guess what, when you wake up, it is again 'today' and tomorrow never really comes.

It is just a compromise. I believe you can do better. There is so much that has changed these days and learning has been made easy. Learning is more about the attitude. Each and every one of us is busy yet some of us find the time to learn new things, for example, one of my clients told me that he walks in the morning for about 40 minutes, 6 days a week. He uses that time to listen to podcasts or a TED talk on his phone. Well there can be many such opportunities that you can grab.

You must also be conscious of the fact that you may have a unique style of learning, some people learn by reading, some by seeing, some by listening and discussing, while some others learn by doing things themselves. Figure out what works best for you. Not every style is for everyone, and you have limited time. It will be best if you find out what works for you and use your time effectively.

LEARNING NEVER ENDS

You learn to gain knowledge and then apply that knowledge to your advantage, doing better at your job, being more effective at work or life in general. You differentiate yourself and get the growth you wanted. Well, then the cycle starts again. Once you get into the new role or position, there will be new things to do, new people to work with and many other new responsibilities. So, then it is time to learn again. As you climb on to the next plateau, your point of view changes and you need to start to look at things differently. Each day you must pick something to learn. Make a conscious effort and before the day ends make of a note of what new thing you learnt today. Every day you miss the entry in your journal is an opportunity lost.

What follows is an inspiring story of a leader for whom learning is a way of life and has been at the core of her professional and personal growth.

****

R. MAHALAKSHMI—LEARNING: A LIFELONG ROMANCE THAT HELPS DELIVER IMPACT

Mahalakshmi comes from a humble background and has continuously evolved over various stints in her career to become a nationally acclaimed leader in the HR space. In her current profile, as Head HR Mondelēz (the Cadbury and Oreo people) she plays a pivotal role in propelling growth for the India business and its people! She is an inspirational speaker and also writes for *Economic Times*, *Times of India* and other key publications. She has a deep interest in coaching, travel, talk therapy and music.

Her experiments with curiosity and learning helped her to grow with every step. Her hunger for learning and her desire for making an impact in the world has kept her pushing forward for more. She has converted her learnings to insights and has applied them in her various roles to create organizational successes. She is always happy to share her hard-earned knowledge and lessons learned, helping others gain unique perspectives.

A Learner from Beginning

Mahalakshmi is an avid reader. She says, '*My early orientation to learning was about knowledge accumulation. I would read a lot, and on all kinds of topics—from fiction and pop-psychology to science. Essentially, I was a "library person." I still remember in school when we could be issued a maximum of one book a week, I would finish that book in a couple of days and request the librarian to give me another book.*' As a child she would unabashedly suggest her uncles and aunts who wanted to get her gifts, to get 'books as gifts'.

She is very grateful to her parents for inculcating in her 'learning by doing'. She remembers that anytime there was a drawing competition, her mother would try and get her to participate. Thinking back, she recollects that it was, perhaps, not that she was a great artist at that time, but by participating she became better at drawing. As she got better, she got more confidence about participating and she learned to put her hand up for many activities.

She says, '*So learning early on was more about knowledge accumulation and putting my hand up to experiences, where I was unknowingly learning. At that time, I never said I want to do dramatics because I want to learn articulation, but I would go for dramatics because it was fun and I would love to dance because it was fun and not because it would give me flexibility.*'

Learning on the Job

After MBA, she started her career in consulting with Noble & Hewitt. Later she joined Arthur Andersen where she learned the basics of consulting, the art of asking powerful questions and the importance of understanding how businesses work. She also understood the importance of engaging with leaders to solve the key business issues rather than implementing theoretical processes, just for the sake of it.

Arthur Andersen only selected the Top 50 Chartered Accountant rankers and she remembers that all her peers were from IIMs or so. Despite being an MBA, she did not have the same pedigree as most of her peers, and she wondered what she could do to be sure that no one regrets hiring her. After some deliberation, she realized that her selection was indicative of some potential and some value Andersen felt that she got on the table basis learnings from her first job. This was her first brush with the realization—that each role, each stint needs to add to your profile and help you to learn and grow. Further, to ensure she lands the impact, she chose a two-pronged approach, the first being hard work and second being observing and learning from others.

The consulting industry also taught her that it is ok not to know everything and today she is not ashamed to say, 'I do not know'.

She has had many opportunities to work on consulting projects where she worked in diverse industries with little knowledge of that industry. Consulting taught her the art of asking questioning to learn in a quick way, what others have learned over the decades. It also taught her the power of connecting dots, and applying learnings from one industry onto another to create new possibilities.

She was also inspired to pay more attention to her personal interests and passions. She fondly remembers one of her managers from the Arthur Andersen, who would plan and take four vacations every year. The manager was passionate about travelling and always made time for it. When the manager came back, she worked day and night to catch up and be up to speed, but she enjoyed her holidays and made space for her passion. It taught Mahalakshmi that if you are passionate about something you can make it work.

Then in India, Arthur Andersen was acquired by Ernst & Young and she continued to work with them in the consulting role for next few years.

The Desire to Make a Difference

The second phase of her career started when she moved out of consulting after about eight years of work experience after the MBA. A lot of her friends were moving out to Global MNCs, but she had different thoughts. She realized that as a mid-level management in a Global MNC, she would perhaps be implementing a lot of global processes and not get a chance to create some of her own. She had a strong desire to create a lasting impact and leave a legacy. She says, '*I thought that the kind of companies where I can get to leave a legacy and where people will really value my inputs as a relative youngster would be large Indian companies. And with that, thought I joined Ranbaxy's R&D unit as their Head for Talent & OD.*'

Her stint with Ranbaxy taught her the importance of learning by having conversations across various levels. This was the first time that she was in an internal HR profile. In a consulting role while one administers surveys to big masses, the one-on-ones are restricted to senior leaders. But the HR role at Ranbaxy taught her that sometimes leaders have a perspective that is limited to what they know, and they may not know grassroots level realities or issues that their people are currently facing. In order to discover what is not really working, it is important to have a dialogue across the levels.

After that she worked for Bharti, a large Indian diversified conglomerate, and initially started at their group office. She did various centre of expertise roles and also played a key role in a large-scale business transformation. She got many opportunities to learn, develop and continue to expand on her abilities. Then she moved to Airtel, the telecom business unit of the company and did various roles there—notably as Global Head of Rewards and then as chief learning officer (CLO) and Global head of Talent. She had retained her childhood orientation of seeking new and sometimes tough tasks for gaining an opportunity to learn. So, when at Airtel, there was an assignment of due diligence in Africa as part of the major global merger, she was perhaps one of the first ones who volunteered to be considered for the task. She says, '*I was doing different roles, and literally every two years I would get rotated to a different world which fed my hunger for learning.*'

She mentions that one of the interesting habits she developed, over these years at Airtel, was self-summarizing things for herself. She claims that she is not really blessed with a photographic memory, so it helped her in many ways to be able to summarize the learnings for later reference. Sometimes, she even makes some drawings to better capture the discussion.

She had taken to Twitter about the time she joined Airtel and had started learning from social media. In a way she believes it is equivalent to learning from your peers, with a potential opportunity to learn from people you have never met. If you follow the right people, for example, somebody who is a global thought leader in his/her own domain, and you read their updates, you may see something that will trigger a new thought or a new idea.

During these days, she came across many inspiring leaders—both within the company as well as from her external network. While business leaders like Akhil Gupta, Sunil Mittal, Manoj Kohli and Gopal Vittal continued to inspire her with their unique approaches to business, she also learnt by observing her HR leaders play the influence game. Equally her external network continued to be a source of inspiration. Top two that she names are Ester Martinez (Head of People Matters—an HR Magazine): a lady who found a blue ocean and leveraged it to create a niche for herself; and Abhijit Bhaduri, who inspires her to stay who you are and pursue creative passions, so as to leave one's unique thumbprint in whatever one does! His journey gives Mahalakshmi the assurance that it is possible to pursue dreams and stay creative (something that she is too!)

Current Role and Learning Beyond the Job

In 2015, Mondelez was looking to turn around and unlock the true growth potential of India business unit. India was the key to the next phase of growth and while the business was growing, it was growing slowly, and the situation was exacerbated with a tough talent situation with the company facing significant attrition and a very high offer reject ratio. Engagement was low and talent felt not invested in. They needed an HR person who could transform the situation and create the right talent strategy. The potential to make a difference drove Mahalakshmi to move to Mumbai. It has been exciting times for her, full of challenges, new experiences and learnings.

She has had the opportunity to learn from coaches and mentors too. She admires the coaches for their ability to come up with those deep and powerful questions that have forced her at times to reflect and even change her thinking or approach about solving a work problem or a life challenge. She has had many mentors as well and they have helped her in many ways: first, by sharing their own experiences; second, by instilling confidence in her own abilities; third, by playing the devil's advocate and challenging her to think more before taking action and fourth, by being great connectors. Even if they did not know the answer, they always knew someone else who did, in effect of broadening her network.

She continues to learn from everyone and one such example is her pantry guy at Mondelez, Abhay. To her, Abhay is like AI (Artificial Intelligence) & CRM (Customer Relationship Management) personalization redefined. There are 60 people on the floor, and he is the single guy who supports all for tea, coffee and stuff. When you are thinking of tea and just as you are about to ask for it, you find that he is already standing next to you with it. He has figured out all the 60 people so well that he knows what type of tea or coffee or when they will need it. His ability to observe, remember, customize and deliver is really amazing.

Her learning has evolved in multiple ways. It is an evolution of multiple sources, the source moving from books to people, to people across levels, to people who are virtual and whom she has not even met. It is also an evolution in learning methods from learning through reading to learning through observation and reflection by participating in projects. She mentions that if you are open to learning, you may create opportunities to challenge yourself by sharing knowledge with others. Especially on the subjects that you are very well versed with. For example, she was at an industry conference, talking about their experiments with digital technology, when people asked a few questions that made her reflect more. There is also the attitude of curiosity which she is quite naturally blessed with. She has an innate nature to enquire and learn.

Learning Helps Her to Deliver Impact

Mahalakshmi says, '*I am in general, a person who is hungry for learning and wish to leave a legacy and make a big visible impact. These are the two things that pretty much define my life choices, and not only my career choices. To me, learning is pretty much like evolution, ongoing learning is the expansion that life needs. Learning is essential for life.*'

She thinks that her two passions are related very closely, because you can deliver impact only when you continue to learn. She says, '*My definition of learning is not training. My definition of learning is having a lot of curiosity for things around you. And learning about organizations, learning about people, learning about how and why of a lot of things, is very important for you to define what you work on and how do you work. So that it becomes meaningful at the end of the day. Therefore, learning is pretty tightly and closely linked to impact.*'

She further adds, '*Gradually as one matures, one also thinks about leading an impactful life, and therefore learning about yourself, perhaps, is as important as learning about others. And learning about the "why" of decisions is perhaps as important as learning about the "what" of the decisions. So yeah, I think in that sense, if I look at it that way, perhaps, learning has been at the heart of my ability to create an impact.*'

Learning Is in Insights and Adaptations

Learning has helped her think more holistically than she did a few years ago. Essentially, learning has given her a variety of perspectives and insights. She says, '*Eventually as a leader, your value is in the insights you bring to the table. Remember it is not in the technical aspects alone.*' She recalls from her days as R&D HR in Ranbaxy, that scientific research without insights could be a failure. She says, '*You can mix the products and see a reaction and you can write it down but insights will only come when you start noticing the changes in the ingredients, and then realize what change in ingredients is causing what output.*' To her, being able to generate those insights, is perhaps the biggest lesson that comes with the ongoing broadening of horizons and widening of perspectives that learning provides to you.

Learning also gives you empathy. When you learn about how people think and what is driving them, you are also able to understand why they behave in a certain way and what are their choices like and so on and that makes it easier for you to relate to all kinds of people. She says, *'Sometimes, watching a movie or a play for that matter impacts you so deeply that it makes you reflect. When you are reflecting, it is for sure that the next decision you take or the next step you make, will be different. So, it is exposing the mind to a variety of thoughts and a variety of perspectives that helps you expand your thinking.'*

And she further adds instinctively, *'And I think, the "art" is in deciding which of those perspectives you want to imbibe and which of that you just enjoy observing but feel that it is not you.'* Learning is not just about the choice somebody can exert, it is also about being aware of those choices.

She also believes that learning has made her an 'asking' leader and not a 'telling' leader. She believes that while a lot of it is situational and though her natural leadership style is to get people together and say, *'Here is what I think, what do you think?'* her learning orientation of including everyone's voice in the solution or even in the articulation of a problem has made her a more inclusive leader. She believes that learning has impacted her decision-making in a similar way, because perspectives are broader. Her decisions come with more empathy and have become more collaborative as she has learned that she does not always have all the answers. She believes that this must be true for all the leaders and as they learn more, their natural decision-making style becomes more collaborative.

Learning makes decisions insightful. She would love to get more time to reflect, because reflection is where learning converts to insight. She believes that there is so much power in stepping back and then reflecting. Had she got the chance to reflect and record her own summaries every time, she could have done an even better job. She believes that reflection gives you time to process the information; the better you process, the finer the result. It helps you in refining and making the result more impactful. Leaders must spare time for reflection.

What Should Organizations Do to Augment Learning?

As an erstwhile CLO, Mahalakshmi believes that the CLO of any organization should not limit their role to identifying and cataloguing the training courses or driving them through the organization. She believes there are two critical ways that the CLO can contribute.

First, the CLO must understand what the organization wants to achieve in future and review if the talent has the skills to realize that vision. The seminal role of CLOs is therefore to identify skill gaps required to achieve that vision. As an example, her current organization wants to 'lead the future of snacking', so the organization needs skills beyond chocolates and confectionery, and need to have people with skills across other snacks. The CLO must work with the business to identify the required skills and then strategize the best way to introduce these capabilities and embed them. This is a combination of exposures, projects, hiring, partnerships and more. So, in her view, the CLO must be the 'capability partner' for the organization.

Second, the CLO must create an environment for learning in the organization. The culture should be such that people ask each other, 'What did you learn today?' They are keen to learn more and if they realize that they are not learning something new, they must recognize that they are losing something. The CLO must make various types of learning resources available to the people. All the roles in the organization must be skill mapped. CLO needs to work with the HR and Business to make sure that the people selected for the roles have the right skills. She believes that a lot of industries seem to be lacking in this space, they have a loose coupling and the skills are not mandatory for getting a specific role. People take them a bit lightly and when they go on trainings, they consider them like a break from work or like a reward and not consider them as value addition. The learning just becomes a fun exercise because they do not have to apply it.

Learning is embedded most deeply when tightly coupled with careers and individual success journey. Learning should not be limited to training but must include jobs, projects, assignments and so on. In fact, it would be best if people could chart their own career path based on their learning needs, as each role that they perform, adds to their comprehension and abilities through application of the trainings and skills. This approach is followed strongly at Mondelēz, through their 'Career Lattices' approach to 'build your own careers'. In fact, they have an annual 'Growing Here Week' where leaders share their career and learning journeys, and inspire teams to reflect on the best way each individual would like to grow.

How Does She Mentor Her Team?

She tries not to be the only mentor for her team and is very conscious about that. She encourages her team to find mentors other than their line manager. Second, she looks out for the relevant moment for sharing learning called a 'coaching' moment. When the incident is fresh, she asks exploratory questions such as 'What do you think happened in the room?' or 'What went well and what could have been better?' or 'What were your observations about what happened to the stakeholder when you were talking?' to help them gain wisdom. She uses her network to expand their horizons, for example at Mondelez, they have some sessions with external speakers each month, thus creating a broader network of learning for the team.

What Mahalakshmi Says about Your Next Promotion

How best should one draw ones learning plans? The mistake most people make is to just focus on their learning gaps for the current role. Mahalakshmi recommends that you need to look at the three pointers.

1. *Your strengths:* Which are your big strengths that you need to develop further to create high impact and shine.

2. *Development opportunities for the current role:* Are there big gaps and opportunity areas you need to work on to deliver high impact in your current role.

3. *Growth objectives:* Abilities required for the future roles you aspire.

Second, people review their learning plan with their manager alone. Your own view or that of your manager's on your development plan may be very different from the view of other stakeholders. If you cannot do a 360 view, you must at least meet three to four key stakeholders and discuss your learning and development plan. That way the plan can be more robust.

Third, once you make a plan, act on it. A plan alone is no good. Set up regular reviews with your

Message for Millennials

Firstly, stay curious and stay hungry and keep challenging the world around you, which, she believes, they do fantastically well. Secondly, she hopes that they can have more patience. She says, 'Touching water will not make you a master swimmer. They jump from one role to the next. I would request them to have the patience to finish learning insights from that experience and finish giving back before jumping to another experience.' In general, she has found that they get bored very easily and potentially like to move from one experience to the next and the next, which may not help in the long run.

manager at least once a quarter and make sure that you make progress on your own commitments. Taking ownership of your plan is the key.

Fourth, find an internal or external mentor to seek help in your career growth. Do not be shy on checking if someone can be your mentor, as sometimes people leave such great opportunities because they assume that the potential mentor will not have time. It will be good if your mentor is a few steps ahead of you and not the extreme master, because it is easier to learn if the gap between the mentor and the mentee is not too much. She suggests making the relationship meaningful for both the parties. You must have some very clear asks each time you meet your mentor, so that you use their time effectively. At the same time, you must try and see what you can do for the mentor that could be in some form of a payback for all the guidance that you are getting.

Fifth, if you are seeking your promotion, you will be evaluated on your leadership abilities, so not just seek a mentor, be a mentor too. Your support could create an impact and get you noticed as well.

She strongly believes that taking the ownership of your development plan is fundamental to your next promotion.

****

WHAT STOPS PEOPLE FROM LEARNING

I would say no one can really stop learning. Every day you learn something, so the question is more about what stops you from learning something that enhances your abilities or potential. Look at the following few reasons and consider if any one of them is stopping you.

I Know It All

You have been contributing to your field of work for decades and you are already recognized as one of the experts in your domain. People seek you out for your thoughts. What more could there be to learn? Also, Malcolm Gladwell in his book *Outliers* said that one needs 10,000 hours or more to be an expert and you have already put in 20,000+.[3] Well, it is not really about what you have already learned. It is about what you can add to it. The capacity to learn is not limited by years or by hours. The music maestros keep on learning new things and keep on innovating or creating new experiences. They do all this in addition to the practice hours they put in each day.

What Can They Teach Me?

You are sometimes working with younger people or people who have much lesser experience in your own domain. You believe that it is your prerogative to teach these people and that there are no possibilities to learn from them. When they show you a new way of doing things, your ego comes in the way and you try and find faults with their methods, rather than learning from them. While they may be able to teach you less compared to what you can teach them, if you keep an open mind the possibility of learning from such an interaction is very real.

This Is Not My Domain

The problems that leaders solve today are multidisciplinary. As no one can be an expert of everything, a cross-functional team is required to work on them. If everyone learns about their own domain and does not know much about the adjacent domains, it falls upon the leader to bridge all the knowledge together. The leader must know something of everything and with each experience the leader must strive to add more knowledge about lesser known subjects. If you aspire to be a leader, you must look at acquiring knowledge which is not only from your own domain.

I Do Not Have Time

If you are too busy chopping trees, you will not get time to sharpen the axe.[4] The truth is that if you stop to sharpen the axe, every so often, cutting the trees will not take as much time. Your effectiveness can increase a lot. I cited a few options for you to find the time to learn in a previous section.

INVOKING THE LEARNER IN YOU

This part is not that difficult, it is a matter of 3 Ds mentioned below.

Desire

You must have a desire to learn. This includes being open during your interactions with others. Have the curiosity of a child. Ask more and tell less. Be open to discover new ways of doing things. Learn from every experience you have. Consider what is the best use of your time and set some learning goals for yourself.

Dedication

Once you set some targets, make sure you achieve them. For example, if you targeted to listen to four talks or podcasts a month, make sure that you achieve this target. The best way to do this is by having an accountability partner, someone who can keep you honest.

Discipline

When you set your goals, you must march towards them at a rhythm, if you falter, you are more likely to miss. You miss once and that becomes a trend. The trick with learning is that it does not immediately transform into results, and there are always other pressing things. You are accountable to just yourself and it is easy to slip. Remember that if you miss, it is your own loss and no one else's. You may not know it today, but you will most definitely feel it tomorrow. So, stay on course. Once you decide on your learning pace, stick to it, maintain a discipline, come what may.

TRANSFORM YOUR MINDSET

A growth mindset will help you keep learning.

FIXED MINDSET	GROWTH MINDSET
I know it all.	There is more to learn.
I have important things to do.	Learning is equally important.
The young do not have the experience to teach.	The young come up with novel thinking.
I need formal trainings.	It is possible to learn from experiences and dialogues.
I only need to learn for my current role.	I must learn more to widen my horizons.

CONTINUOUS LEARNING: IN ACTION

The following few questions will help you to reflect on learning.

- What are the three roles that appeal to you? (These must be the roles that you can take up with your next promotion.)

- What are the skills and attributes required for those roles? Seek out people who are doing those roles, observe them and if possible, have a chat with them to learn what are the key skills and attributes required to be successful in those roles.

- What are the gaps from your current abilities?

- What resources will be required? Chart out a learning plan.

- Who can help you on your plan?

- Who can be your accountability partner?

- What time slots in your week can be dedicated to learning?

It's what you learn after you know it all that counts.

Harry S Truman

REFERENCES

1. TED. *Quick list of all TED talks*. Available from: https://www.ted.com/talks/quick-list [Accessed 14 February 2020].

2. Medium. 5-Hour Rule: If you're not spending 5 hours per week learning, you're being irresponsible. *Accelerated Intelligence*. Available from: https://medium.com/accelerated-intelligence/the-5-hour-rule-if-youre-not-spending-5-hours-per-week-learning-you-re-being-irresponsible-791c3f185e6 [Accessed 14 February 2020].

3. Gladwell M. *Outliers: The story of success*. Boston, MA: Little, Brown and Company.

4. Lincoln A. *Quote attributed to Abraham Lincoln*. Available from: https://www.brainyquote.com/quotes/abraham_lincoln_109275 [Accessed 14 February 2020].

10

IT IS OKAY TO ASK

❝ ❞

Don't be afraid to ask questions. Don't be afraid to ask for help when you need it. I do that every day. Asking for help isn't a sign of weakness, it's a sign of strength. It shows you have the courage to admit when you don't know something, and to learn something new.

BARACK OBAMA

If the thought of asking makes you feel nervous, anxious, lesser, shy, you could be missing out on some amazing opportunities. Reflecting on my own behaviours, I realize I had also apprehensions about asking when I was in a corporate role. I have now had the opportunity to speak to so many people who have had similar thoughts on asking.

One of my clients from a large IT organization shared sometime back that she always wanted to go on an international assignment and had never got the opportunity. Exploring further with her, she shared that she had never specifically asked her management about it. She just assumed that the opportunity will be given to her as a recognition of her good work. She was delivering on all the metrics and was managing her team well but getting frustrated that she was not getting that chance. The thing she was missing was 'asking'. She had not even considered 'asking' as an option.

Many people get stuck in their roles or levels because they do not ask for help or an opportunity. If you are stuck at the plateau, it is important to present your 'ask' to the relevant people at an appropriate time.

ASKING IS NATURAL

Questions come to our mind all the time and as humans we are naturally curious. In fact, our entire learning experiences are designed based on two facets: listening or reading and then asking. Today, we have an option to learn virtually, yet many of us may love to join a live class for an opportunity to interact and ask questions. To ask is human.

ASKING IS MADE A CHALLENGE

Children are relatively free with their queries; they ask a lot of questions but as they grow up, they become self-conscious. Also, the adults sometimes push back by saying things like, 'I thought you already knew this'. This associates the feeling of 'shame' with asking and slowly pulls one away from it. No one likes to be laughed at or made fun of. We learn not to ask some things in the public for the fear of embarrassing ourselves, our family or others involved. Then we learn that some things cannot be asked, they need to be guessed. Asking in formal set-up becomes more complicated and it starts becoming a big thing. To keep things simple, we start making a lot of assumptions, especially assumptions that are known only to us. This becomes a way of life and we start expanding the sphere of assumptions.

THE MOST DIFFICULT 'ASK'

Asking is relatively easy if you want to know about some details of a project assigned to you. It is also easy to ask if you have some doubts about what you just heard. It is ok, if it is clarifications that you are seeking. But it is difficult if it is a favour you need.

You worry what will happen to your reputation or self-image in case your request is turned down. It becomes easy if you have to seek a favour from a friend. It becomes difficult if you have to seek a favour from unknown people. It is a different case when you seek favours on behalf of someone else. You have got less to lose, and it does not feel so difficult. Sales professionals do it all the time, they seek favours or ask for commitments on behalf of the organizations they represent, and they are quite ok with it.

The most difficult thing to ask for, is the one that you believe you already deserve. Let us say that you believe you deserve the promotion and feel that the leadership must give it to you. Asking in such a case becomes tough, as you feel you deserve it and for some reason it is being denied to you. You feel that asking will not make a difference because all you may get are some excuses for the denial.

WHO WILL ASK, IF NOT YOU?

What happens when you stop asking for yourself and wait for things to happen on their own? The nature of things is such that if you show no desire, you may be perceived as less deserving. This can become a vicious cycle. You may miss many opportunities just because you shied away from asking. You are the master of your own career and you will be failing yourself if you delay the 'ask' or sometimes neglect to even consider it.

THE ASK IS NOT ONLY ABOUT YOU

The denial of an 'ask' is not a feedback on your potential, it only reflects the state of affairs at that point of time. It is also about what is possible. The dialogue gives you the chance to know the conditions under which that 'ask' can become a reality. Once you are able to hammer out an agreement, you will know what to do. The other person in the discussion becomes a partner in your journey if the requirements are defined in the meeting. Remember when you raise the ask for yourself, you give yourself a chance to succeed.

Sometimes your ask may result into changes for a lot of the other people too, who have not had the courage to speak for themselves. That is where the leaders are born, they take ownership of the success of all involved and take it upon themselves to become the voice of countless others. They look at things and seek to make improvements, they question, and they ask and work to make things happen.

An ask is also about understanding the perspective of others. It is also about listening. Quite a few times things may not turn out to be in the exact same fashion that you envisaged. When you listen and understand, new ways can be forged, and things can still happen in your favour.

Let us read the story of a leader who raised many asks and enabled many others in her wake.

****

APURVA PUROHIT: ONE OF THE MOST POWERFUL WOMEN IN BUSINESS

Apurva is the president of Jagran Group and leads multiple organizations, including *Dainik Jagran*, *Mid Day*, *Inext* and *Inquilab* along with India's first private FM radio station—Radio City. She is the author of two popular books, *Lady, You're Not a Man! The Adventures of a Woman at Work* and *Lady, You're the Boss*. Her books have been translated into multiple languages. She is on the board of a few organizations as an independent director. Apurva is a thought leader in the space of 'diversity at work', 'women empowerment' and 'women leadership'. She has been ranked as one of the 'Most Powerful Women in Business' as per the India Today Group for 2016 and 2018 and Fortune India in the year 2018.

Her journey had many challenges, but she overcame them all, and broke the glass ceiling to become an influential leader. Today, she is a beacon of hope for millions of aspirants. Like any successful leader, she has had to earn her place and many times during her career journey, she had to ask for what she deserved. This is the story of her journey to that coveted leadership spot.

Early Signs of a Bright Career

As a child, she was an introvert by nature. She was very intelligent and always excelled in studies. Apurva says that her mother is an intellectual and an overachiever, with genius-level IQ. Her mother noticed in the early days that Apurva was doing brilliantly and was hardworking compared to her peers. She believed in Apurva's potential and kept on pushing her to achieve more and more. Although those days there was limited awareness of all the possibilities of higher studies, her mother was determined that Apurva should complete her MBA from one of the IIMs, the best management schools in India. Apurva did not get into engineering unlike most of her peers because she planned to spend more of her time preparing for the MBA studies. Throughout her graduation, her mother kept on motivating her to work hard and achieve her goal. Apurva got selected in IIM Bangalore and she tasted the very first of the successes.

Facing the Real World

She had lived a very focused and protected life till college and IIM was a whole new environment for her. She faced multiple challenges in the very first year of the MBA. She had always been one of the brightest students and her self-confidence was built on her intelligence and abilities. When she joined IIM, she was surrounded by 150 bright individuals and some of them also had years of experience to boast. She started to lose confidence in her abilities. She remembers an incident when she had to speak extempore on a subject in front of the whole class within the first week. She could not speak at all and she spent her five minutes silently and awkwardly. This incident further hurt her, and her grades started to suffer. This became a vicious cycle that threatened to pull her down.

Then she happened to do an internship with an advertising agency, Rediffusion, and things changed for her. She gives credit to her mentor at Rediffusion who worked with her and pushed her to do better each day. Fortunately for her, her summer project with Rediffusion went so well that she got a pre-placement offer in 1988. In the pre-liberalization era, good jobs were rare even for the IIM students, so this was a great confidence booster for her. The work that she did over these two months of the internship was instrumental in getting her to believe in her abilities again. She realized that she was good at what she did. She had a new learning; that the external circumstances cannot affect her inner abilities. She reflected and found that she had let the experience, intelligence and abilities of others to make her feel less. Once she put faith in her abilities again, she started doing well and finished the second year of the MBA with great results.

She started to love the creativity, brand thinking and was naturally driven to marketing as a subject. She became quite determined that after the completion of the MBA, she will go into advertising. In 1989, she started her career journey with Rediffusion and it became the foundation of her successful career. She has since then picked up roles where she could blend business and creativity or roles which were based on marketing and advertising and challenged the creative side of her genius.

The Confident Professional

Most of the IIM students did not join advertising those days because the average salary they paid was around 60 per cent of what an MBA student would otherwise get. Just three out of her batch joined advertising. She chose to join Rediffusion, which was a marquee advertising organization that used to win many creative awards. What attracted her to Rediffusion was the whole mix of the strategy and creativity and the opportunity to work with so many brands at any given point in time. It was a role which demanded both the right-brain and left-brain type of activities and was very engaging and satisfying.

Her assignments included business discussions with the customers for creating the brand strategy and collaboration with the creative people within the organization to develop the marketing campaigns. First 4–5 years broadly went into advertising-related work, though at some point she moved from Rediffusion to FCB-Ulka. She loved her job and worked with a lot of confidence and soon she was promoted to be a manager and recognized as a leader. What differentiated her from others was that she had much lesser hesitation compared to other colleagues. She would say her mind and would not worry too much about 'what others would think or say'. And though she was an introvert, she would not shy when it came to work. This characteristic helped her table more ideas and experiment more and become even more self-confident. With a string of successful projects, she built personal equity in the organization.

In the year 1993, she had her first child and she looked out for a part-time job to cope with the family responsibilities. That was the time she got into a discussion with her organization and raised an 'ask' saying, '*I told the management that though I want to work with the organization, I may not be able to continue in my current profile for a year or so. That I can only work for 3–4 hours of a working day and not do the extra hours that the profile during those days demanded. I sought other options for myself and asked them for an alternate work that I could do.*' Since she had her previous reputation supporting her, she was able to seek this favour. And they came up with the option of a role in the 'Media' side of the business, which was more like a desk job where she could do some flexi timing. That was way back in 1993 when such things were quite unheard off. She 'asked', and she got it. In fact, she pioneered a new support model for women at FCB-Ulka. The changes that triggered because of her 'ask', became a policy which made the life for other women easier in her wake. Even today, FCB-Ulka is recognized as one of the best places for women to work.

Looking back, she thinks that four things worked in her favour as she made that important ask: first, she had worked hard and established a good image; second, she was good at her work and was producing results. It was not just hard work and loyalty. Third, when she said that she will be able to work only for three quarters of the day, her manager believed that because of her efficiency she would still be doing more work than her colleagues and last, she had a female manager, one who could easily relate to Apurva's need to be with her kid for more time. She says that her manager supported her at the time of her need.

Less than 30 and Heading a Business!

Her role in media planning was interesting in its own way as it was a new thing. It was less creative compared to advertising but had its own charm. Media planning and buying were just picking up as a concept in the country. She made sure that she did justice to the new job and worked hard though she put in fewer hours than before. Her efforts bore results and she can recall her leaders recognizing that what she managed to do in part of the day could easily be a two-day work for others in the organization.

Because of her experience, early exposure and hard work, she was able to create a lot of successes and continuously expanded her work. In recognition of her successes, she was promoted many times. Eventually, she became the head of a business vertical at the age of 28, when she started a new subsidiary company called

Lodestar UM for FCB-Ulka. Lodestar UM is one of the largest media agencies in the country even today. She was heavily engaged in this business for about seven years and then she got the next big break.

A Young President

In 2001, at the age of 35, she was offered the role of the President of ZEE TV. From media head to be the first CEO and President in her batch, she had got a big jump. She had joined ZEE when they were going through the tough times. STAR TV had come into the country and had taken up a leadership position and ZEE was being challenged. ZEE was also going through a lot of transformation at the leadership level, but she worked relentlessly for the next two years and they managed to stabilize the business.

In 2003, she accepted another challenge to set up the TV channels for *The Times of India*. She went through a new phase where she had the opportunity to learn a lot in terms of setting up the TV channels business from scratch, including taking the relevant licenses, buying the transponders, setting up the infrastructure of the newsroom, choosing and prioritizing channels, selecting and launching brands, recruiting a star anchor such as Arnab Goswami and so on. She worked hard and drove for results, but as goes with leadership positions in larger organizations, as she got deeper into the expansion, she found most of her time went into nurturing agreements and seeking alignments rather than the blend of creativity and business that she was passionate about. Though she learned a lot in that experience, it was quite 'draining', and she was losing her steam. She sought out a change.

She says, '*In 30 years of my career, I have not been required to create a CV even once, though I have changed roles many times. I believe that because I had built the right credibility, I had been able to get an opportunity to change every time*

I asked for one and sometimes even before I asked.' When you build a great image and great relationships, you may not even need to formalize your ask, people know it instinctively and you get things even before you ask.

Back to Her Passion of Creative Businesses

A private equity firm had just bought Radio City, an Indian FM Channel, and they were looking for a senior professional to lead this new business. They reached out to Apurva. The role excited her, and she happily accepted it. Apurva says, *'The advantage of running Radio City was that I had the free hand to set up and run the business. Unlike my previous roles, I now reported into a board and was in the driving seat for the business. I asked for what I needed, and I got what I asked for. It was freedom with responsibility, business and creativity, a heady mix that I love so much.'* She did this role from 2005 to 2015, for about 10 years, and cherishes the period as the best phase of her career.

When the private equity firm exited in 2015, Apurva was approached by the new buyer Jagran Group to run the multiple businesses that they owned. She saw this as the next phase of her career. In her previous roles, she had learned about setting the right cultures, the right processes, challenging the teams to achieve goals and keep moving the needle on business while being creative and insightful. Now, with this new profile, she had the chance to work with multiple CEOs on their own journey to excellence. She worked with Jagran Board to create the right position for herself. She was quite clear about what she wanted, and she articulated her ask to the Jagran Board and finally got the role as well as the compensation that she believed she deserved. She began a new phase of her career where she now managed multiple businesses each with their own CEO. She has been in this profile since 2015 and is making a difference, every day.

When She Hesitated to 'Ask'

One area she believes she missed 'asking' early enough is about the knowledge of the digital world. As she assumed leadership roles and the organizations got more and more digital, she found that her juniors were savvier than her. But she hesitated to ask them about their knowledge, believing that she must put this effort on her own. She worried that asking may reduce her position in their eyes. She says, '*As a leader, you must not burden yourself with the fact that you must know everything, you will always have team members who are better than you in something or the other.*'

She loves to 'self-talk' and reflect. She thought long and acknowledged that the lack of digital knowledge is a lacuna that she needed to eradicate. While she had resources in her own team that could help her, her own hesitation was stopping her. She eventually got over it, as her need to be successful in every project she undertook, took precedence. She left behind the hesitation and formalized her ask for learning from her team. In the hindsight, she believes that she would have benefitted from asking earlier and has never repeated the same mistake of delaying the ask. Today, she is one of the best leaders among her peers on the knowledge of digital. In fact, she has used digital strategy to the advantage of the organizations she leads.

Another example from her career when she did not 'ask' was when she helped secure new buyers for an investor-managed organization that she was working for. Ideally, she should have got a 'finders-fee', but she could not ask, as she felt odd asking for the fee. She was hoping all along that it happens naturally on its own course without her explicitly asking for it. If a third party had arranged for the deal, they would have definitely got the fee. She felt bad about it and had wondered, '*Why the investors are not paying this to me? Is it fair?*' She believes she could have done better at that time.

Asking Is Not Limited to Office

Your professional success does not depend only upon your hard work and contributions at office. The single-minded focus that you bring to the office is built upon the foundation of a great support at home and this is true especially for the women professionals. Even Indra Nooyi has said that women professionals have to build their own safety net. Apurva was keen to continue her profession when she became a mother. She asked for flexi timing from her office and got it, but it would have all been for naught if her mother had not agreed to support her. When Apurva asked for help with raising her son, her mother agreed and left her own job to support Apurva.

As she continued to make progress at the office and got into bigger roles, she started getting a lot of pressure. She had greater expectations about maintaining an impeccable home and it fell upon her to take care of this part. But soon she realized that while she still desired the outcome, she could not shoulder the complete burden of making it happen. She asked for greater support from her husband. He stepped up and took a greater role in parenting and even increased his participation in household activities. Now that her son has grown up, she has enrolled him for help many times. Her ability to ask from her family has helped her pursue her career with great vigour.

What Stops People from Asking

Apurva says first, we always compare the potential upside and downside of an action before deciding to follow the course. If the downside is bigger, we normally decide not to act. Before asking for something, you may fear rejection and consider that as a big downside. Apurva believes that the fear of rejection could just be in your own mind and may not be a reality. There is no harm in asking. At the worst, your 'ask' may be rejected, and you can find yourself at the same place you started. But you must remember

192

that there are chances that a dialogue may start, and you may get what you asked.

Second, she believes that you may shy away from asking because you are afraid that you do not meet the expectations for asking. And she thinks that you may feel insecure if you know that you have some shortcoming that you could have done better, that you have somehow been a bit of a slacker and wonder if you would be challenged when you ask.

No organization wants to lose a good employee and they would listen to your ask. She earlier quoted the example of her demand for flexi timing but there could be other examples, such as asking for a promotion or a role change. She elaborates further with an example, '*Let us say that you are working in corporate communications, but you believe you are good at brand marketing too. You can go ahead and ask for it.*'

What Can Organizations Do?

Apurva believes that good organizations teach collaboration and teamwork well. One of the pieces of effective collaboration is advocacy and inquiry, where you advocate your point of view and also enquire through appropriate and empathetic questioning. The key is to understand other person's point of view. Quite a few times, people just make some assumptions about other person's motivations. This leads to inefficient discussions, delayed decisions, misunderstandings and costs the organizations a lot. Organizations need to facilitate people in learning a key lesson in asking, which is about learning to 'ask' to understand the other person's perspective and context before presenting your own 'ask' or requirement.

Apurva claims that leaders continue to build on their innate curiosity to develop their skill of 'asking'. To quote from her book *Lady, You're the Boss*, '*Behind the air of self-importance that most leaders carry, lies a thoughtful and—most importantly—curious nature. They question the status quo and look beneath the hood to see why the engine is working or why it is sputtering. They probe, they question endlessly, and they are restless in their quest for more information and knowledge.'*

She believed that people may get emotionally attached to their own ask and their own perspective of the situation and may fail to ask about the other person's thoughts. They may fail to recognize that the power of the discussion lies in creating solutions that they personally would not have thought about. The 'ask' that they raise during the discussion may not materialize in the fashion that they requested, but a new way could emerge.

The truth is that these are difficult skills to learn and the organizations must align mentors for their high potential people to help them learn and grow.

How Does She Mentor Her Team on It?

'Asking' is a difficult skill to learn. Apurva mentors her team by using a two-pronged approach.

First, she leads by example. This she believes is the best method to make them learn. They get inspired when they see her asking for their opinions, even when she has different perspectives. They learn when they see her being open to accepting other alternatives that work for all.

Second, she shares with them the lessons for making a good ask. For example, before asking for the next promotion, people need to ask themselves first whether they are ready for the next promotion? Have they prepared themselves for that role? Have they watched and mirrored their manager? Have they learned to think at the next level? How ready are they for the next set of responsibilities? Only if the answers to these questions are yes, they should make the 'ask' a formal request to the management.

What Apurva Says about Your Next Promotion

She says asking has two steps, the first step is 'Asking-Inside' when you use yourself as a sounding board and determine if you have done a thorough job in your current role and that you are ready to deliver on the next role that you are asking. She has examples from her organization when people who want to become a CEO shadow the current one for a substantial period of time and learn about multiple functions before they believe themselves ready to ask her for the role for themselves. She also has examples from the other end of the spectrum, where someone keeps on asking for the role even though they do not have the skills required for the next role. One such case is of an individual who is doing great in their current role and missing on the key skills of collaboration required for the next role. The individual is not aware of the new requirements and mistakenly believes that he/she is ready. Unfortunately, your ignorance is no excuse and the leaders in the organization are not likely to grant your ask.

Also, at this point it is prudent to know if what you are asking is feasible, let us say you are seeking a foreign assignment and there are no open positions. If you present your ask without determining what is possible, you may just waste a chance. It is desirable that you explore and determine what is the best thing that you must ask for and make sure that you are prepared to support your claim.

Once you are convinced that others will have confidence in you, you can go to the second step, that is, 'Asking-Outside' and formalize your request with the competent authority. If you feel you are not ready for 'Asking-Outside', then you must ask yourself, what you can do better to make yourself ready for the next step. Apurva is quite sure that you can always find the right answers if you look hard enough.

Apurva also says that 'asking' is a game of mind. If you believe that you will become smaller by asking or that you will be looked down upon, you will shy away from asking. You must respect yourself and believe in yourself. If you do not believe in your self-worth, others will sense it in your ask. You must truly believe that you are 'worth it'. Once you communicate your ask with that belief in your mind, others are more likely to agree with you.

She says that 'Organizational Context' is another aspect that she wants you to be conscious of. What if you tabled your ask and it was granted too! Is there a way that you can still fail? She says the

> ## Message for Millennials
>
> Millennials are very different from earlier generations. They have grown up in an era of plenty, with instantaneous information and responses at their fingertips. They have a lot of confidence. This means that they find it incredibly easy to ask or stand up for their rights. Because they have also learned to navigate diverse sets of circumstances and people, they know how to ask too. My only advice would be that they should learn patience. Sometimes results happen over a period of time, and just pushing may not translate into success.

answer could be 'yes' if you miss the organizational context. She has an example; a person in her organization became aware of a bigger role that was available, she staked her claim and even negotiated for a good salary. The organization was going through a transformation and over time the role got diminished. At one point, she was asked to go as she did not fit into any other available role. She missed the organizational context and asked for a role that had a short-term relevance. If you miss the context, you may be asking for more than the environment can afford. You may get something under pressure, but it may not work out for you.

Apurva believes that knowing how to ask and having the courage to ask is great but waiting for the right time to ask is important too, as building your own equity takes time. Asking involves the building of trust between the two people who are involved in the discussion. Consistency and dependability are important in addition to smartness and agility.

****

WHY ASKING SEEMS DIFFICULT?

Let us explore some aspects that may discourage you from asking.

Fear of Asking

Many of us have been raised with a belief that if you ask, you may not look smart enough or worthy enough. Some of my clients have shared experiences where they relate asking to 'being vulnerable'. It is an unsafe space for them. Another related belief is, 'I got to do this all by myself.' That is the way, some people perceive, it works. Fear comes from these beliefs. One of my clients was made an interim CEO and was struggling to meet the expectations. He was still handling his previous role and was not able to do justice to the job and feared that he might fail. Once he shed his hesitation and started asking for support from his team, former peers and board members, he started making great progress.

Fear of Miscommunication

The second most common fear is that you may not be able to convey your point in the right way or that the other person will misunderstand you and their perception of you will change in a negative way. In some situations, you may also think that asking something could probably offend the other person. Do remember that asking for someone's help is a sign of respect.

Fear of Feedback

Many are apprehensive of the feedback. They are afraid that they may not like the feedback and shy away from asking.

Getting Out of Comfort Zone

Asking is certainly getting out of your comfort zone. You are afraid of what you do not yet know. When the outcome of the 'ask' can either benefit or hurt you, you do not want to venture in too close to the outcome. Requesting others to consider your 'ask' may seem uncomfortable.

Law of Assumption

A few times, you just assume that the other person will understand the situation in the same way and that stops you from asking the right things at the right time. The assumption stays your hand and stops you from discussing all the options.

Trust

When there is no trust in a relationship, asking can be scary and uncomfortable. You may need to work on building enough trust to be able to ask comfortably.

HOW TO ASK?

Asking may need guts, but only the first few times, then it starts to flow with ease. There are many things that you can do to make asking easy and simple. Asking is like a muscle—you must flex it, use it, to strengthen it. Consider the following few pointers, each one of them will help you to become better at asking.

- *Prepare yourself in advance:* Do your homework. Think about what you are going to say.

- *Know the 'Why?' of your ask:* If you understand the 'Why?' clearly, you will increase your chances of presenting yourself more confidently and concisely.

- *Set the context right:* Do not beat around the bush. Set the context of the conversation clearly in the meeting. It is always easier to communicate when the expectations are set properly.

- *The right thing at the right time:* Timing is important. You must find the right moment to ask. Understanding of the situation and the people helps you to ask things at the right time.

- *Design your ask:* It is important that you have adequate clarity in what you want, and that the articulation of the ask is quite simple and straightforward. It pays to renew your accountability and commitment, just to add sincerity to your ask. Add facts and data if applicable. Do not downplay your achievements, highlight them. Also talk about the impact your 'ask' is going to have on the project, team, business or organization at large and so on.

- *Be realistic:* Your 'ask' must be feasible. You must know about the constraints or limitations posed by the organizational structures and rules. Your 'ask' should be within the framework. Remember you can stretch the fabric of the organization but not break it.

- *Your EI and conversational intelligence will come handy:* Make sure you are not getting too emotional about the 'ask'. It is in the professional context that you are relating your 'ask'. Manage your emotions well; your articulation must be logical. You must choose the right emotions to exhibit, for example, while asking for promotion, you must not sound frustrated or upset. You should sound excited and eager to take on more.

- *Asking is a conversation:* Listen and let others speak too. It is about yourself, but not all about yourself. If you listen well, you will learn a new thing or two and will probably discover more ways to reinforce your 'ask' over subsequent conversations.

- *Practicing the 'ask' conversation can help:* If you have a mentor or a coach, you can practice your 'ask' with them. That will give you some ideas about potential reactions and will help you prepare.

- *Do not stop if the answer is a 'no':* One of the answers could be 'no' and that should not deter you from 'asking' in the future. You must give yourself credit. Asking is about you, but the immediate result of the conversation is not about you. You may be deserving, but it may not be the right time because of so many reasons. So, give yourself the credit for asking, thinking through it and making an awareness about your needs. Learn from your discussion and work on making your 'ask' even more compelling the next time. Keep doing what you are doing and that too with high quality even if the answer is not a clear 'yes' at that point of time. Follow up if needed. You can also check with the other person, when it will be a good time to revisit the topic. Keep working on the 'ask', do not quit.

TRANSFORM YOUR MINDSET

Embrace the growth mindset always.

FIXED MINDSET	GROWTH MINDSET
I will not be able to ask for this.	How can I put forward my 'ask'?
How can he say 'no' to me?	Let me understand the reasons why he said 'no'.
I do not think she will even listen to my 'ask'.	How can I present my 'ask' that she listens to it?
She judged me when I asked for help.	People are different and so are their perceptions. Let me understand her perspective.
I am working hard here, why should I even ask for my promotion.	It is my career, let me see how I can convey my thoughts.

ASKING: IN ACTION

The following few questions will help you to reflect on 'asking'.

- What do you want to ask?

- How feasible is it?

- Who are the stakeholders involved in the discussion?

- How much you know and understand them?

- What is the right time to ask?

- What makes you think your 'ask' is important to them?

- What are the facts and data you have to support your 'ask'?

- What are your emotions when you are thinking about the 'ask'?

- What are the emotions when you are thinking about the meeting you are going to have?

- What can prepare you more for the discussion?

- What will you do if the answer is a 'no'?

One who never asks either knows everything or nothing.

Malcolm Forbes

11

DIVERSITY AND CULTURAL INTELLIGENCE

66 99

We are all different, which is great because we are all unique. Without diversity life would be very boring.

CATHERINE PULSIFER

Diversity has been recognized as one of the pillars of success for the organizations and there is a lot of discussion going on in the industry about using diversity to strengthen the organizations. In today's fast-moving business world, diversity of thought and ideas lead to much needed creativity and innovation. In global organizations, cultural diversity is also an important consideration. Every organization has a different culture, and each business unit may have some unique cultural elements. To reap the benefits of a globally diverse workforce, the leaders need to be culturally sensitive. If you are not conscious, you might create hurdles for your own growth.

NEW LEADERSHIP IMPERATIVE

The new age leaders respect diversity and promote inclusion.

- They make efforts to promote diversity in hiring and make sure that the hiring process is unbiased.

- They encourage inclusion by making sure that the voices of diversity are heard and that everyone participates in the decision-making processes. They set a culture that promotes harmony and cooperation within their team.

- They are aware of the strengths that each diverse group brings to the table and leverage those strengths to create success.

- They leverage the differences to help the organization move its charter forward.

- They build the right bonds such that all the diverse groups within the team extend all the possible support.

DIVERSITY IS INTEGRAL TO SUCCESS

It is very natural to be comfortable with people who are most like you. But believe me, you may not need more people who are just like you in your team.

Imagine a cricket team with everyone good at batting or imagine an orchestra with just violin players. You cannot create a symphony with just one instrument or one type of talent; you need diversity in the right mix. You need a team of people who complement each other. Once you have the right team set up, imagine the number of symphonies that you can create. Innovation and creativity come from either venturing into unknown or by learning new ways due to inadvertent mistakes committed by someone. A diverse team is bound to be more creative and innovative. These two things will keep you and your organization ahead of the curve and are the new currency of success.

Diversity also helps to improve the decision-making in your team. It has been proven by a research that diverse groups outperform the individual decision-makers by a significant margin.[1] One person, however great a thinker he or she may be, will still fall short of a collective effort at problem solving. Let us consider an analogy from sports; a cricket team with great batsmen cannot hope to win against a team that has balanced performance across batting, balling, fielding and wicket-keeping. Having diverse skills and perspectives will help you think better and wider, preparing better for all sorts of contingencies and ensuring success despite changing circumstances.

Research has also proven that as the workplace becomes more inclusive, employee engagement increases, and attrition reduces.[2] This also results in better employer branding and provides access to better talent.

ARE YOU REALLY GOOD AT IT?

Most of the times, leaders may not get any direct negative feedback from the team as it is a sensitive topic. In a round-table discussion that I was a part of, a manager shared that he was devastated when he got a feedback from HR that some team members are uncomfortable working with him. He believed he had been humorous and worked closely with the team, while the HR received complaints about certain jokes being targeted at a community. His team had never raised any concern with him, and they had always laughed with him.

Lack of direct feedback is no evidence that you are doing good on diversity and inclusion. You should carefully reflect upon various conversations with your stakeholders to sense any feedback. If you feel the need, initiate a specific dialogue to seek more details.

EVERY LEADER NEEDS GLOBAL SKILLS

Gender diversity, age diversity, etc. are quite different from cultural diversity. You may be a leader of a diverse team in your own country but when you take up a role that spans beyond one country, you will encounter newer dimensions of the diversity.

There are no guarantees that the skills that you have so far will be able to help you to manage these newer dimensions. And you may not be able to get clear guidelines to help you be successful. You need to work hard, make the extra effort and forge those human connections that span all types of diversities. You need to make others comfortable with you, have engaging dialogues and you need to listen deeply. Once you discover what needs to be done, you can then make quick progress.

> *When we listen and celebrate what is both common and different, we become a wiser, more inclusive, and better organization.*
>
> **Pat Wadors**

Let us now read the experiences of a leader, who worked in different geographies and had team members from all over the world while serving customers in 50+ countries. Let us learn from these experiences and gain some insights to building this crucial ability.

****

ASHLEY PASSOW: PSYCHOLOGY OF DIVERSITY AND CULTURAL SENSITIVITY

Ashley is a global leader at Accenture and has deep expertise in enabling the Fortune 500 companies to meet their talent management goals. She has led multiple large-scale global projects affecting 150,000+ people at a time. Working with global diverse teams has taught her so much, including the power of embracing all people as equals.

Ashley's first job was in high school at Starbucks in 1994 where she had the opportunity to serve a variety of people. She says, *'I think it is really important that everybody experiences some sort of a job serving the public. You learn a lot about how to interact with different people.*

If somebody is having a bad day, they can be grouchy about how they are ordering their cup of coffee. I really had to learn that if someone is not treating me as I would expect, it is that person's issue and not because of something I did. Initially I took these things personally, but then I learned how to manage them and it ultimately helped me to be stronger. I also really enjoyed serving bright cheery warm people and knew then that those are the people I want to use as my example and be like them.' She still uses that as a way to live her life and works to treat all human beings with respect.

This is the story of Ashley's journey as she worked in different roles and learned new things about working with people from around the world. She shares her lessons from her experiences with diversity.

Early Career

Ashley went to the University of Colorado and achieved a degree in psychology. She chose psychology because she was always fascinated with how people think and what motivates them. She was also intrigued by how different people can contribute differently, and how individuals have endless potential. She wanted to learn about how to help people achieve their potential.

In 2000, she got a job at a small training and development company in the city of Boulder where she wore many hats. Working in that company she learned a lot about sales, the learning industry and working with different types of people.

A Project with an Overseas Team

In 2004, she was excited to join Accenture in her role as an instructional designer developing courses on many different topics including SAP training. She quickly learned that it is not possible to know everything and figuring out where to find the information and skills is what enables success. She also learned the power of working for excellent leaders and how important it is to ask for help—a skill that is critical regardless of where someone sits in an organization. This is where she developed her own passion for leadership and management.

Her next project provided her an opportunity to work with people in Bengaluru (India)—a culture that Ashley deeply admires and respects. This was also the beginning of Accenture starting to partner with people in India on such a large scale. Ashley found it interesting because many US-based companies were very US-centric at that point, and she learned a lot about working with diverse global teams. Ashley learnt the value of cultural intelligence and providing the right context to the diverse teams there.

Ashley very much values time with family and friends, especially when celebrating holidays. Before she was aware of the major holidays in India like Diwali, she had inadvertently asked the team in India to work on some of those weekends too, due to some critical deadlines. Once she found out what had happened, she was devastated that they worked during that time and took that as a lesson to learn about someone's culture at the beginning of the working relationship.

The other main skill she learned was helping people have the right context of a situation so that they can understand the unified big picture. Due to geography, people in Bengaluru would only see some pieces of the complete task. As a result, they were at a disadvantage relating how it all worked together. She realized that in some respects, the lack of context and understanding was preventing the team in India from doing their best. She worked with the teams to help them see how their work impacted the larger initiative and the quality of output significantly increased, as did team morale.

Communication is the key and everybody has different words, styles and ways of presenting ideas. Initially it was easy to think that people from a different part of the world were not speaking in an unfamiliar way, resulting in a communication gap. The truth was that they had a different way of phrasing things and she had to learn their style and that they had to learn her style. Together they went through a learning curve. But when she invested the time and effort to understand how they worked, she started making progress towards being on the same page and having a proper context in place, ensuring success for all.

Working Abroad

In 2007, an opportunity to go to the UK and work on a project in financial services in Ireland came up. She remembers sitting in the conference room discussing the challenges in that project. Somebody was required to go out and help, and she just raised her hand. She says, '*I felt I can do it. I had no idea what it really meant or what it would need but the idea of trying something new and different was really exciting to me. And I think that was one of the things that differentiated me from my peers; my willingness to take on the challenging assignments.*'

When she moved to the UK, she herself experienced some instances of stereotyping about Americans. The team was fearful and guarded around her and this put her in an awkward position. She wanted to make people comfortable and invested a lot of her initial time and energy getting to know them as individuals. Only when people started to get to know her, they realized that she was there to help. Through this journey, she recognized how important it is to build rapport with colleagues and get to know one another and build trust.

This was another interesting multicultural assignment, as she was working in UK with the team developing content for a company with the help of a team from India. They were trying to develop sales training. The India team was understandably not familiar with the European culture and they did not have context.

Understanding of each other's perspective was not working across the various global teams. Her job was to help connect those dots. She says, '*I found it challenging but also really inspiring because everybody is driven by the same things, that is, they want to have fun with each other, they want to earn money to take care of their families and they want to grow their careers. So even though everybody had a different culture and point of view, the ability to bridge those gaps to me was really exciting and fulfilling.*'

She quotes another example from this time about diversity that is related to practices about annual holidays. In her experience, in the USA, people did not frequently take long holidays. In the first half of the year when people in her UK team started taking two or three-week holidays, she was really frustrated, because she was concerned about moving the work forward. After living there for some time, she started realizing that people performed better when they had more breaks, especially long breaks. It is beneficial for not just the individual, but the organization and society as well. Going on holidays was a part of their culture, which was a key part of the culture she eventually embraced.

Ashley has had many positive influences in her career. During her time in the UK, she acknowledges her mentor Eloise Price who had an impact on her outlook on life. Eloise is British and has lived in Singapore and to this day is traveling all over the world. Ashley admires how she gracefully manages people with warmth, understanding and care. Eloise's global experiences and demeanour enables her to make everything feel very easy and open, even when times are tense, challenging and stressful. Ashley acknowledges that Eloise is such a wonderful role model on how to respect all people and to treat them as equals.

After a year of living in the English countryside she was given an offer to be the global curriculum lead for another client and she moved to London to lead that team. On that team, she had people from Brazil, Argentina, UK, South Africa and from all over the world working for her, designing curriculums and learning strategies for approximately 50 countries. With her learnings, and because of the diversity on her team, they worked well together and continued to innovate and grow.

A Role Away from Business and Back

In 2014, she had her first son and went on maternity leave. She moved back to the USA because she wanted to be closer to family. When she came back to work, she picked up a role in HR. It allowed her time with her son. While that time was great, she quickly learned about her passion for being client-focused. She says, '*Even though I had fewer working hours, I missed working with clients, so I moved back into client delivery work and that is where I am in my current role where I lead a global account team. I am happier working longer hours because I find the work engaging and feel like I am growing in my career.*'

She continues to lead global learning and development initiatives in her current role with a focus on technology companies in Silicon Valley. While she remains focused on the theme of innovation, she stretches much further these days beyond digital learning, into the world of analytics. She strongly believes that the future is in being data savvy so that the team can prove the return on investment. She is really enjoying her new role and team.

Ashley is now an acclaimed professional and is a proud mother of two sons.

Diversity and Cultural Sensitivity

Ashley says, '*Diversity is incredibly important, and it is not just so that we can have the stamp and say we have the metrics. Diverse teams bring new ideas, new ways of thinking, allow us to have better products and frankly, it makes work more interesting.*'

She has a fundamental belief that all humans are created equal and all humans want the same thing: health and happiness for themselves and their family. If you approach people from that perspective, it goes a long way in working through conflict and enabling you to negotiate with others and find mutually acceptable solutions. However, if you believe that one culture is superior or one race is superior then you may approach the things with a subtle bias, which prevents coming to common terms and common answers. To find solutions, you have to step back and see it from other person's perspective.

She believes it is easy to get stuck in the mentality, '*This is how something has always been done, so therefore will always be done.*' The more people you talk to, the more you learn different ways to do things. Her husband is from the UK and they have been together for 10 years. One of her favourite things about being in a marriage with two cultures is that it challenges her assumptions about how things should be done. Such experiences expand the mind and enable us to consider other options that ultimately improve life.

To Ashley, diversity is not just about race and gender. It is much broader than that, it is diversity of ideas, it is also about different age groups, preferences and cultures. It is important to embrace it all. To her, it is more about the feeling, 'I am unique'. It is always about the other person's unique individual perspective and the thoughts that they can bring to the table.

Cultural sensitivity has a lot to do with the willingness to understand another person and you must educate yourself and your children on cultural differences. She again gives an example from her own marriage and the fact that she lived in the UK. There are generalizations about both the British and American cultures. And while some of those stereotypes can be true, there are many examples to prove otherwise. If you are traveling to a new country or location, being aware of customs and cultures goes a long way to being able to build relationships and trust with people.

She had an opportunity to work with global teams and had to adapt to be successful in the diverse cultures. The first thing that she learned is to be patient and understanding. She really makes sure that she understands what the other person is saying, by slowing down, as well as seeing it from their point of view. It helps to ask a lot of questions versus being somebody who knows it all. The second part is her willingness to travel and meet people in person. While she is a big fan of virtual working, she believes human connections are invaluable. She has seen this with her clients as well. When she was having a hard time getting agreement on something, it was amazing to see what she could achieve just sitting down over dinner or drinks as human beings together.

She strongly believes that diversity in age groups is key. Experienced people bring a perspective having lived through challenges and similar scenarios in the past. Take advantage of these learnings. Younger people out of school have a fresh perspective and see the world through a different lens that enables them to offer new ideas. Neither should be dismissed and both are necessary for society and business to thrive.

Unconscious bias is also a problem at the workplace. '*Everybody has some unconscious bias, yet they will say, I am the most open person and everyone else has a problem. All individuals were taught beliefs that are deeply ingrained and are nearly impossible to lose. There are cultural norms that are ingrained in us. What matters is how we hold ourselves accountable for being aware of these biases so that we can then work through them.*' One's own environment shapes beliefs. Getting real examples and getting to know people also goes a long way and that is where she feels lucky that she has been able to travel and work with people from all around the world.

What Can Organizations Do to Promote Diversity?

Ashley spends the majority of her time working virtually. That said, she meets the team in person as frequently as time and budget allow. For virtual global diverse teams to be successful, team members need to meet people in person and build those relationships. Organizations must invest the time and money required for this travel as it goes a long way in improving the satisfaction of the people and makes a global team successful.

Hiring for diversity is important. People like to hire people who look like themselves, but it is important that we deliberately hire people who approach things differently. It starts with recruitment but is also about how you build and blend teams. Creating a blended, diverse team is important, as is taking 'unconscious bias' training. She has personally learned a lot about herself through that training and has seen that this training is effective on teams and organizations.

She believes that organizations must explicitly educate people to improve cultural sensitivity. For example, if someone is going to be working with the team in another country, they must be taught about that country's customs. It may be very basic like some people celebrate Christmas and others celebrate Diwali. It helps to understand so that you do not make comments that might come off accidentally to be rude, even if you do not intend them to be.

How She Mentors Her Team

Ashley tries to avoid general comments, such as 'that is just how the (name your group here—Americans/English/French, etc.) are'. She does not like her team members talking down about groups holistically. Travel is a luxury, but something she encourages if people can afford it as it expands horizons and enriches life. She conducts multiple activities like Global All-Hands and she does things like trivia to help team members learn about their colleagues' cultures, and she also offers opportunities for people to present about themselves. They share things about family, the holidays they celebrate, types of vacations they go on, what their house looks like and so on. Then the team gets to know the individual even though they are in a virtual environment and may not meet in person. These activities are important for creating sensitivity about diversity.

What Ashley Says about Your Next Promotion

Ashley believes that you should surround yourself with diverse people so that you discover different ideas, thoughts and ways of working, which will enable you to be innovative. Innovative people are going to get ahead and you make it so much easier on yourself when you have got a network of people you can go to. The more diverse that network is, the more successful you are going to be.

Second, everyone needs to have sales skills and knowing how to sell is important. Whether you are an engineer, interior designer, doctor or a business person, you have to be able to sell your ideas. To be able to sell to someone, you need to see things from their point of view. Today, you are selling to people from around the world. You need to understand the different cultural norms and points of views and individual perspectives to be able to sell and be successful.

She believes that what gets you to the manager level is different than what gets you to senior leadership level. Getting up to the manager level it is all about how you manage your teams, how you do project plans to deliver quality output on time. What gets you promoted to executive level is also your ability to manage upwards. Executives are very smart, busy and powerful people. They need to feel a connection to you and trust you. Develop that trust by understanding issues from their point of view, quickly get them answers and demonstrate your ability to think critically to help solve problems. It goes back to the point about the network and the way you grow it by surrounding yourself with people having different ideas and different thoughts. If you have a more diverse network, it pretty much guarantees your success. She says, *'There's a lot going on at Accenture. We have about 500,000 people and there is no way I could know everything. I am very much an expert in my area, and I know who to go to in order to find answers which goes a long way in me being successful.'*

> ### *Message for Millennials*
> Ashley thinks millennials may be a lot more open than previous generations, so they have got a 'Head Start'. They embrace diversity and run with it. Millennials bring a lot of strengths to the table around diversity exposure to various cultures and spread this knowledge to others in a kind and helpful way. Millennials use technology to connect globally, but they must know when to step back from it and establish human-to-human connections.

She encourages you to embrace diversity in every possible way you can, to help you get to the next level.

****

DIVERSITY IS AN ACQUIRED SKILL

Quite a few times, the diversity initiatives by the organizations produce lukewarm response. It may seem easier to continue with business as usual and ignore this specific element. That said, there are couple of basic issues that hold people back.

Human Bias

Our beliefs and intuitions have been built over the years. Our own environments help shape them. New things seem wrong sometimes and difficult at other times. Just to dig a little deeper, consider the fact that some part of the world uses left-hand driving and the other uses right-hand driving. Neither of them is wrong, but for people used to one system, it is quite difficult to instinctively act in the other.

Letter versus Spirit

Many initiatives are implemented in letter based on organizational guidelines. This happens when the management does not spend time to make clear the benefits of diversity to individual leaders and managers. People are also unlike to embrace diversity when the organization does not dig deeper into details to come up with organization-specific policies and they just copy and paste something that has worked well for someone else.

Ownership

Leaders may not take ownership of such initiatives as they may believe that it is over and above their usual business responsibilities. As long as they are able to produce results with the current team structure, they may hesitate to topple the apple cart.

WHAT CAN YOU DO?

Appreciating diversity will help create a safe environment for employees and promote higher performance for the diverse teams you have. You lead by example.

Recognize Your Biases

As always, the first point is to be aware of your biases. Feedback can help if you are open to it. You need to take very specific feed-back about the biases and beliefs you hold. It will show up as your behaviour and attitude towards others. Operating with an aware-ness of diversity will help you to be non-judgemental. You will be able to see it as a positive thing. No amount of training can help you do it unless you are aware and willing. Watch out for your drivers. What is driving you to seek diversity? Genuineness is very important.

Do Not Judge People, Understand Them

You will agree with me that we all have some preconceived notions about people depending on how they look, which country or which part of the country they belong to, which language they speak and so on. We judge them without even being aware that we are doing it. We prefer looking at people with our lens. There is a need to understand people and respect them.

Get the Required Knowledge

Do your homework before getting into a new geography. Do not assume things. Value systems are different but even similar values are expressed differently in different cultures. Every culture will say we are kind, but the expression and extent would be different. You need to observe and listen to understand people before you colour them with your own perceptions. Reading books and watching a foreign language movie can be a good start. Put yourself out there in that space and start interacting with diverse set of people, you may soon become aware that other people are thinking differently. One way to do this is by having conversations or dialogues about culture and values with colleagues who have different backgrounds. You should develop a capability to work with cross-cultural people for achieving best results and performance.

Showcase It

Cross-cultural competency is a skill that may not come naturally. You may have to work with your mind-blocks and beliefs. You need to be caring, compassionate, empathetic and sensitive about feelings, ideas and thoughts of others. You need to start by showcasing that you care. You should verbalize your intent and seek support from others involved to help improve the situation. Make sure that you do not compromise your own values. Use the dialogue to showcase your values and help others understand your actions. Diversity is a two-way street; every time you take one step forward, you also need to make sure that others take a step of their own.

Align Your Thoughts to Organization's Values

Most of the organizations have values which clearly respect diversity. When in doubt, always align to the organization's values. Reach out to the HR primes for help when you need.

TRANSFORM YOUR MINDSET

Change is tough and a fixed mindset stop us from developing.

FIXED MINDSET	GROWTH MINDSET
Millennials will not understand this.	Millennials are a different generation, let me help them understand my perspective.
People in that culture always do this.	Every culture is different, I must respect their practices.
We do not have anything in common.	Let me initiate a dialogue to discover common elements.
I believe this task can only be done by this group of people or a gender.	Let me see how I can have a more diverse team for this task?
It is a difficult task to work with so many cultures.	It is a great opportunity to learn by working with different cultures.

DIVERSITY: IN ACTION

The following few questions will help you to reflect on diversity.

- What do you think of your acceptance of diversity?
- Who have you taken the feedback from?

- Write your biases and reflect on your behaviours due to them.

- What can you do about these biases?

- How will increasing diversity help you?

- What actions can you take to improve inclusion in your team?

- Who can help you?

A diverse mix of voices leads to better discussions, decisions, and outcomes for everyone.

Sundar Pichai

REFERENCES

1. PM Editorial. Diversity drives better decisions. *People Management.* Available from: https://www.peoplemanagement.co.uk/experts/research/diversity-drives-better-decisions [Accessed 14 February 2020].

2. Caitlyn Pittman. Diversity & Inclusion can Boost Employee Engagement. Rewardian. Available from: http://blog.rewardian.com/diversity-inclusion [Accessed 14 February 2020].

12

EMOTIONAL INTELLIGENCE

66 99

*What really matters for success, character, happiness
and life long achievements is a definite set of
emotional skills—your EQ—not just purely cognitive
abilities that are measured by conventional IQ tests.*

DANIEL GOLEMAN

'Emotional intelligence (EI)' has been a buzz word for more than a decade now. In simple words, EI is your ability to be aware of your own emotions and the ability to manage your emotions well. It also is your ability to be aware of other people's emotions and enables you to empathize with them. A good grasp of EI will help you to improve your performance across all the facets of your professional life and help you to utilize all other skills in a better way. It would not be wrong to say that it is the secret code for success at work for all the professionals especially beyond mid-level management.

At the same time, it is one of those skills which are good to discuss and easy to relate to but difficult to imbibe. It may well be possible that most of the leaders that you have ever hated were low on EI.

HIGH CORRELATION WITH SUCCESS

Many prominent research houses have been building a body of knowledge and proof through years of research to prove that EI matters and that there is a high degree of correlation with professional success. More and more employers are recognizing this fact. While some have already included some form of evaluation as part of the hiring process, others look for some evidence as part of the interview process. A career-builder survey of more than 2,600 hiring managers and HR professional established the importance that employers lay on EI.[1] More than two-thirds said that they valued EI over IQ in general, and three-fourths said that they are more likely to promote an employee with high EI.

In 2017, a study was published in the *Journal of Vocational Behaviour*, which claimed that people who are high on EI earned more over a decade than those less in tune with their feelings.[2] The study also stated that this effect is stronger at higher organizational levels than at lower levels. The results suggest that EI helps individuals to acquire the social capital needed to be successful in their careers.

WHAT DOES IT ALL MEAN?

As much as 80% of adult 'success' comes from EQ.

Daniel Goleman

EI entails a lot of stuff which happens inside you and others. It takes time for you to understand it and observe its manifestation on the outside. Daniel Goleman has published many books on it and the four-quadrant model that he provided is the simplest way to contemplate the dimensions of EI.[3] The elements of this model are given below.

1. *Self-awareness*: The first component is to recognize your own emotions and how they affect your thoughts and behaviour.

2. *Self-management*: The second component is to be able to control the impulsive feelings and behaviours and manage the emotions in healthy ways.

3. *Social awareness*: The third component is to have empathy to understand the emotions and concerns of other people. This will provide you the ability to identify emotional cues of individuals and dynamics of the groups.

4. *Relationship management*: The fourth component is to develop and maintain good relationships and working well in teams by communicating clearly, inspiring and influencing others and managing conflict.

UNDERSTANDING YOUR EMOTIONAL INTELLIGENCE

When people do not have high EI,

1. They do not regard or respect themselves well enough. One of the examples is that when somebody pays them a compliment, they underplay their own contribution.

2. They do not empathize and relate to others. They tend not to understand the other person's situation or needs. They communicate bad news directly and assume that all others will be able to manage. They do not take the time to make the other person understand.

3. When somebody shares a feedback, they either ignore it or become defensive and feel that the person is not aware of the hardships that they went through.

4. They mix professional and personal life in a stressful way.

5. They are not able to give enough attention to the issue at hand. While people are talking to them, their mind is somewhere else.

6. When in meetings, they are not able to understand emotional dynamics in the meeting room.

7. They feel stressful in normal day-to-day situations.

8. They keep feeling bad about somebody's behaviour or action, etc. on most of the days.

While this not an exhaustive list, it gives you an idea to reflect on. The reflections will help to understand what is happening with you at an emotional level.

HOW DOES HAVING A GOOD EI HELP YOU

The people skills associated with EI are crucial, because people are an important part of any business. Awareness of your own emotions and that of others is important to stay focused and lead effectively.

Some key reasons why organizations prefer top leaders to have great skills on EI are:

1. Nobody wants a stressed or emotionally dull executive. The former will scare people away and the latter will fail to motivate teams.

2. Decision making is incomplete without considering the emotions. A leader who is aware of his/her own and other's emotions knows which of the information he/she needs to utilize or omit in order to make better decisions. Even when you need to influence others, if you are able to relate to people, it helps you to articulate your thoughts in the best possible way. Many studies suggest that leaders who are emotionally intelligent are able to defuse tense situations and make better decisions ensuring that they take people along.

3. Relationship management is better with EI. Executives and leadership team works with very diverse set of people, such as Investment Bankers, Founders, Analysts, Customer leadership teams, Designers, Programmers and so on. They need to learn to understand the emotions of these people to be able to relate to them and work closely with them.

4. EI provides you with the ability to engage and lead teams. EI also helps you communicate more effectively. By being aware of the emotions, you would be able to choose the right moment, the right words, the right tone, etc. to put people at ease.

5. Once you actively listen to your team, it will be easier to empathize with them. You can read the situation much better and it is easier to share bad news too.

Daniel Goleman said that the most effective leaders are all alike in one crucial way. They all have a high degree of EI. He says IQ and technical skills are important too, but they are table stakes. So, everyone who gets the leadership role, already has the knowledge and the experience. What differentiates a great leader from a good one is their ability to relate to self and others.[4]

****

AMANDEEP GUPTA: A CHARISMATIC LEADER'S JOURNEY TO TRANSFORM HR AND BUSINESSES

Amandeep started as an engineering graduate and moved into the world of HR. He had a difficult start and rose up to overcome the challenges, learning a lot in the process and scoring many victories. Learning became an integral part of his journey and he continued to evolve as a leader. He has been instrumental in transforming HR practices, organizations and businesses. Currently as the managing director of the Trident Group, he believes in the power of getting the people strategy right. There is a lot that we can learn from his inspiring story. Let us look for the words of wisdom hidden in his tale.

Shifting Goals

Amandeep graduated from Thapar Institute of Engineering and Technology in 1990 and like many other youngsters at that time was aspiring to get into Civil Services (Indian Administrative Services). He took up a job in Delhi and also started preparing for Civil Services exam. However, he soon got engaged in his work and could not devote enough time to the preparations. After a few months, he decided to join Thapar Institute as a lecturer so that he could get more time to prepare. But as luck would have it, he could not clear the Civil Services and in 1996, he decided to pursue a job in the corporate sector. He believed that teaching was not utilizing his full potential and that he could do much more.

As it was difficult to get a corporate job after the teaching assignment, he initially struggled to get back. He finally got the role of a deputy manager, training and development, at Ballarpur Industries Limited (BILT). Typically, the training and development departments are led by people with an MBA specialization in HR, so he was an exception to the norm. The way he embraced this role and the way he evolved himself over the next few years, contributed a lot to his own growth as a professional and a business leader. His ability to grasp various practical business aspects and the ability to relate to people made a huge difference to his success.

Embracing the Fear of Failure

He struggled a lot initially in his new job as he did not have any HR experience to rely on. He was the youngest deputy manager and faced resistance initially as many people did not accept him or his ideas.

He was reporting to the Head of HR for the factory. He remembers that in his initial days, one of his colleagues was being non-cooperative and never gave him time or support. Amandeep took these conflicts to his heart and this affected his confidence and performance. About six months into his job, he got the news that his probation may get extended as his performance was not meeting expectations. He had never failed earlier, had always done great in academics and wanted to succeed desperately in this job too. In a moment of self-reflection, he acknowledged the strength of his qualification and ability to find another job in case the need arose. Once he conquered the fear of failure, he performed better. For him, it was a do-or-die situation and he made all-out efforts to create a difference. He started figuring out his way around the problems and problematic people and thus, started to taste success.

First Learnings on People and Behaviour

He feels extremely lucky to have had Tapan Mitra as his manager at BILT. He saw Tapan dealing with the worker's union, employees as well a few difficult people. Amandeep being young at that time used to question Tapan as to why he gave importance to such difficult people. Tapan explained to Amandeep, in simple terms, that if he wanted to know people, he should listen and try to understand what they were going through.

He says, *'Tapan taught me by example. He used to have unlimited patience when he was listening to someone who had a grievance. Even though it was none of his fault, Tapan would take it upon himself to put the person at ease.'* Subsequently, Amandeep realized that Tapan's greatest asset was his EI.

Working with Tapan, Amandeep learned that

- He needed to accept people as they were and not overly focus on the fact that they liked him or not.

- He needed to focus on the problems they were facing and work on solving them, making their lives easier.

He says, '*If you have differences with someone, you should definitely let them be known. Though you must strive to de-link them from the person and must not discuss with any emotional baggage. You should focus on the problem and the best way to make it work for both the parties. If you cannot be completely objective, it is still better to discuss the issues, rather than leave them to fester in your side.*'

With these learnings in mind, over time he started delivering great results. These early challenges and learnings made him a people's person and he started developing his people skills in a big way. Over time, Amandeep learned to respond and not react. He learned to listen, take a pause, digest, empathize and then respond. Though he realizes, that by innate nature he is very spontaneous, he says, '*Even today when the environment is positive, and we are talking about business, I am very spontaneous, and I do not hold myself back. At that time, I rely on my creativity and authenticity. But when the discussions go down to negative and let us say that we are discussing about somebody's poor performance or we are discussing about negative behaviours, then I take a pause. I think and reflect before I express my opinion.*'

High-Potential Performer

BILT set up employee assessment centres and Amandeep was identified as one of the high potentials. He got promoted, got put on an accelerated growth path, got transferred to Delhi and was made part of the team that was responsible for ERP transformation. This was a hand-picked team of just 12 people, with one representative from each function. This experience gave him true business learning. This team was a '360 degree' business team and had the mandate to understand the business processes, map them onto a requirement and then identify the best fit ERP solution that BILT should implement.

As he spent time understanding the business, he started realizing the vastness and complexity of it all as well as the interdependencies of various functions. This helped him a lot to deliver better in his HR role.

The Learner in Him

He did not have a formal MBA degree, so he kept learning through various HR forums and platforms. He vividly remembers an HBR article which solidified the importance of EI and other managerial competencies. As per the article, in the beginning of one's career, whatever function you are working in, technical or functional competency (function of IQ) has disproportionately higher impact for delivering in the role. However, as you move up in the organization's hierarchy, the role and impact of EQ keeps on increasing.

This really hit him, and he started paying a lot of attention to managerial competencies. In hindsight he further adds, '*Emotional intelligence to me means that you do not react to things, you respond to them. That means, before you react, you process the stimuli, you give it a thought, you become empathetic to the person or the cause of the stimuli and then you choose a course of action that is not intended to hurt others but to improve the situation. Nobody wants to do something wrong intentionally and that we need to understand their situation before reacting. I do not speak to people when I am angry with them. That does not mean I do not express my anger, I do, but I do it only when I am not in the state of anger.*'

He also adds that, '*An important aspect of emotional intelligence is the fact that you are aware of your own emotions. If I do not realize that I am angry, how will I stop myself from saying hurtful things to others. So, I have learned to discover my own emotional state. The fact that I realize that I am angry or getting angry reduces the anger a lot. It makes me better prepared to respond positively.*'

Fast Track to Be the Head of HR

In 2003, he was approached to take up the role of Head of HR at Bausch & Lomb. It was a transformational role and an orbit shift for him. It was a great experience for him to be a part of the Executive Leadership team. He was responsible for all key decisions as well as efficient execution. He developed deep listening skills and realized that empathy was one of his key strengths. Most people who know Amandeep really well, especially his wife, say that when people talk to him, they feel at ease with his words. He comes across as an approachable, non-threatening and non-judgemental person. He believes that in the leadership roles, these things are critical. Especially as you grow higher in the Indian hierarchical system, if you do not make yourself approachable, there will be an invisible wall around you and people will stay away. It is the leader's responsibility to demolish the wall.

He was doing so well at Bausch & Lomb in India that he got some responsibilities outside India as well. In 2006, he was offered the Group Head of HR role in Dalmia Cement, an organization five times bigger than Bausch & Lomb in India. This spurred him on the next phase of growth in his career.

Making a Big Organization Even Bigger

Amandeep believes that this was one of the best career moves he ever made. Dalmia Cement was at an inflection point because at the time of his joining, a transition was happening. A new leader, who was from the next generation of the promoter's family was taking over the management and was in the process of charting a new course for the business. Amandeep became a sounding board for the new leader as he had the relevant experience to provide valuable insights.

In Bausch & Lomb, the majority of the strategic decisions were taken in either Hong Kong or Rochester and the India team was mainly focused on the execution. For Dalmia, Amandeep was in fact, sitting in the headquarters, a place where all the decisions were made. He was part of an exciting journey for the organization, charting a course of growth from a market cap of about ₹500 crore to about

₹25,000 crores, and the turnover growth from ₹500 crores to over ₹12,000 crores.

Amandeep is proud to say that over time, his role expanded to include corporate communications, corporate affairs, administration and so on. Eventually, he also started looking into the business aspects of the organization. He says, '*When organizations hire individuals, they do have a profile in mind such as Head of HR, Head of finance and so on; however, a lot depends on the individual that gets hired. If the individual is more capable than the role, he or she starts expanding the role and contributes in multiple areas. On the other hand, if the individual hired is less capable, the role itself starts shrinking. You will find that in some organizations the head of finance is only taking care of accounting while in other organizations the head of finance or the CFO is also taking care of MIS, Investor Relationship and may also be overseeing IT functions of the organization.*'

One of the other mentors that Amandeep acknowledges is Hema Ravichandran. She was Head of HR for Infosys in its growth phase. Hema was his coach and mentor from 2008 to 2012. During this period, he had completely transformed the organization from HR perspective. Some of the big-ticket changes he carried out were—changing from six days a week to five days a week, adding lunch facility at factory, moving away from salary and benefits to CTC and so on. One of the key learnings from his interaction with Hema was that he needed to be more inclusive as he went through these big changes. He sought suggestions and listened. If there was merit in the suggestions, he would willingly incorporate the suggestions in the policy roll out. This again made him more people centric and an inclusive leader. He believes that such guidance over the years helped him completely transform and become an 'aware' Leader.

Starting Afresh and Repeating Success Once Again

One of the group companies under the Dalmia industries, was a company called OCL. He joined OCL as Joint CEO in December

2011 and later became the CEO. During his tenure, he helped the organization grow from ₹1,800 crores to more than ₹4,000 crores in six years, doubling up the sales and profits in the process.

As Amandeep picked up this new job, he worked hard and worked long hours for the first two years of being the CEO. He had to learn a lot of new aspects of the business as a whole. But once he was able to build the right team, he started delegating the jobs and things became smooth again. These two areas—building teams and delegating effectively, have always been his strength. He has been using delegation with extreme efficiency. Though he had been practicing the art of delegation for years now, he believes he could not have articulated delegation as simply and comprehensively as he can do today. He says, *'Delegation to me means the fact that you should not do any job that one of your team members can do. Even today when any new task comes to my desk, I quickly send it to the person in my team, who has the ability to do it. Only if I can find no one, I pick the task myself.'*

People-Connect Is the Key

Amandeep says that his skills in EI were not always what they are today. He started relating to the word 'emotional intelligence' much later in career, when he was already a general manager in HR. However, he always related to people better than his colleagues at all levels of roles he had done. For Amandeep, people are more than an 'entry' in an excel sheet, he had an innate ability to relate to them. He says, in the older days, all the data entry into the HR database was manual and people made mistakes in data entry all the time, even simple mistakes such as documenting 'male' for a female candidate or vice versa. He says, *'I always wondered how people can make such mistakes. If they treat other people more than just a line in an excel sheet, they would do a much better job. We must give more importance to the data related to people. A single mistake can impact them badly. We must be serious about all such work.'*

He further says, '*I did not have a background of cement, or for that matter finance or sales. I have the ability to pick the right people for the right jobs and the ability to make sure that my vision for the business also becomes their vision. I am always there to support the people when they try new things and make sure that they know that I have their back if something goes wrong. I say credit is yours, debit is mine. People see you doing it not once but again and again till the time they develop absolute faith in you. Then they give their best to you, and they never doubt you again. They go all-out to make things happen.*'

On the aspect of developing people, Amandeep really goes by one of Gallup's recommendations that says do not just focus on your weaknesses, the majority of your time should be spent on developing your strengths. He says if we have complementary skills in the team, with the right grouping we can get the best out of the team and each can play to their strengths and contribute in a better capacity. The efficiency of the whole system improves significantly, and you have more happy and effective employees. However, he points out that a leader needs to take special cognizance of the weaknesses that cause damage to the organization and harm other employees. If an employee is being very political or is spreading misinformation, it is not to be tolerated. Direct feedback must be given, and employee must be asked to take corrective action. Not to act in such scenarios is a serious failure of leadership.

Another thing Amandeep takes pride on is that no one from his team has ever resigned on him. His ability to find the right people, enable them, empower them, has always helped him to connect with them in the best possible ways. The level of trust he has with his team is exemplary and has always helped him achieve extraordinary results. His promise to his people is that, '*Each month, or each year that you spend with me, your skills and your abilities will be better than the last. Your competence will be better than the previous year. You will do something that you have not done before. And if you are ready to do, you will also do something that you think you cannot do. I would not promise you top notch salaries, but my promise is that*' *you will have a good career with good compensation and most importantly, you will enjoy your work.'*

The Right Mindset

Amandeep acknowledges the fact, that as human beings we all have a tendency to judge people. However, over the years he has learned to not have a fixed mindset. He recalls that when he was the head of HR, Dalmia Cement, he was called by the recruitment head to interview a candidate. When Amandeep saw that the candidate was busy chatting casually with another person, he felt that this guy may not be good for them, he seems like he does not care about the importance of the interview. So, he went into the interview with a negative but open mindset. After a few questions he was able to change his opinion about the person. They hired him and he did great. Amandeep suggests that even if you cannot overcome the habit of being judgemental, you must keep an open mind.

He believes that for a growth mindset, you must be open to receiving feedback. He says, *'Be open to feedback from people around you, especially those who have your best interest in their mind. Be open to change, do not have a fixed mindset. Treat feedback as a gift. Many people do not like to give feedback and they have to really go out of their comfort level to provide it. Realize that the feedback is for your benefit.'*

He refrains from saying anything bad about anybody behind their back. He has made this as an important rule. He prefers to share the negative feedback directly with the person himself/herself. He treats this feedback as a gift for them and uses it to provide a way for the person to develop.

How Can Someone Know If They Are Emotionally Intelligent?

Amandeep has his own litmus test for it. He believes that if people are unhappy about their situation and believe that the world is unfair to them and is not the best place to be, etc., it generally means that their EI is low. The world is equally unfair to all, even to the colleague who sits next to you and laughs with delight at small incidents. If you have EI, you will make the best of your life, not be sad about it and waste it by complaining about it.

What Can Organizations Do?

It starts from the top. Today, there will be no leader who is not aware of EI or the importance of it. But do they exhibit EI? HR must make sure that they act as a mirror for the leadership teams. Firstly, they can have assessments organized so that people can know about their own competence and secondly, they can create development opportunities through trainings and coaching. But they cannot do much if people do not take the initiative themselves. While HR can be an enabler, you are the one who is responsible for yourself.

How Does He Mentors His Team?

He does three things.

First, he coaches them.

Second, if they get upset, he gives them space.

Third, he acts as a role model. When situations are upsetting, he does not react badly; he sets right examples.

When people work with him, they start becoming emotionally intelligent, whether they realize it or not.

What Amandeep Says for Your Next Promotion

He believes the answer to developing EI is simple. If you really want to develop, you must have a coach. You must believe in the coach and take the right actions. Nothing will happen unless you act. EI is like developing a muscle, you must practice. You can usually not walk alone. Having a coach can greatly speed up the learning and help you develop faster.

In the current trends of nuclear families, the lack of human interaction from early childhood hampers the development of EI. Growth of social media continues to hamper the development of EI in the youth. You must go out and work with real people, friends, family to become emotionally intelligent. The more your experiences, the better you become. He says that the wisdom he has gained is the result of years of practice and hard work as well as a tendency to seek feedback and guidance from coaches and mentors and taking that as a genuine gift for self-development.

He believes that all mid-level managers must realize that EI is a must for getting into the leadership roles. He says, '*Professional competency is like a passport. You must have a passport to travel to the USA. But is that enough? The answer is No! One must also have a visa. And EI is the visa. Not everyone who has the passport gets the visa. You must qualify for it and deserve it.*'

Amandeep believes in three-step process for becoming better at getting the 'visa'.

- Know Yourself— Lead Yourself

- Know Others— Lead Others

- Know Business— Lead Business

He says, '*Most of the people I come across, do not even know themselves. Only those who know themselves can lead themselves. And only those who can*

Message for Millennials

Amandeep has a couple of suggestions for Millennials.

First, slowdown! If you want to achieve more in life, just slowdown.

Second, if you want to become good at emotional intelligence, work on it, practice it. Only by practice can you become good at something. One cannot learn tennis by reading books on it or by listening to podcasts on tennis.

lead themselves, can also lead others.' You must first realize that you need EI, and then you must identify the gaps, and work on them.

Amandeep believes that there is a lot of strength in being aware of the emotions. This awareness may be the difference between a knee jerk reaction and a reasonable response. If done properly and consistently, it establishes yourself as a leader, a dependable leader in all sorts of circumstances and paves the way for your growth.

****

CHALLENGES THAT PEOPLE FACE

There are quite a few things that stop people from being emotionally intelligent, but here are three prominent ones for your consideration.

Lack of Self-awareness

Consider a math equation as

$$35 + 40 = 90$$

If you are asked to correct it, most probably the answer that comes to your mind is

$$35 + 40 = 75$$

While this is not wrong, it is the way we are programmed. Every time we see an equation that has a problem, we correct the 'right' side of it. The following answers are also correct and possible.

$$35 - 55 = 90$$

$$35 + 40 + 15 = 90$$

And there can be many other possible solutions, but we tend of think of only one.

In daily life, when we face challenges and disagreements, our solution typically involves changing all the others. In our mind, we become right and everyone else becomes wrong. The part where you ignore any potential changes in your own self is the biggest hurdle for EI. You must remember that you are also a part of the equation and you must be self-aware.

You Are in a Hurry

You want to get things done, quickly. You know one way of doing them and see any discussion to change, a challenge to your authority. You fail to listen, you hate to have those dialogues for improvements, you want to just push on. Discussions are not explorations, they are a power tussle. If you are stronger you prevail. Else, you accept and move on. Emotional clouding leaves no room for empathy for others.

It Is Intangible

In the short run, it is difficult to measure the results of your efforts. Therefore, it may be easy to ignore the emotional aspects at work.

WHAT CAN YOU DO?

Your own emotions come in your way and shape your world view. If you are able to determine that you need to strengthen your EI skills, you can work on them by observing yourself in action and then reflecting upon your own behaviours. The following three will help you take the steps in the right direction.

Seek Feedback

Ask others about their feeling when they are with you. You will have to create a safe environment to get this information, as normally people would only talk good. You can also get some anonymous 360-degree surveys done to get this piece of crucial information.

Once you know how you make others feel, you can then consider ways of improving their experience.

Reflect on Your Behaviour

At the end of each day, take a note of your best meeting and your worst one. Consider your feelings in each of them and reflect upon the factors that helped create that feeling. Note these triggers and be aware of them.

Hold Back during Extreme Feelings

Do not let yourself react during the time that you are angry or upset. Note down your response but delay it. When the worst moments have passed, review your response, consider what could be a constructive way of bringing out your thoughts and reframe the response.

TRANSFORM YOUR MINDSET

Enhance your EI by imbibing the growth mindset.

FIXED MINDSET	GROWTH MINDSET
This is about business, what have emotions got to do with it.	Human beings have emotions and they produce best results when they feel understood.
I need results, I do not care if the team is unhappy.	Results matter, but team happiness is important too.
Others do not understand me.	I may need to cool down and think objectively.
One bad news can spoil my day.	I can accept bad news and work towards solutions.
I cannot fail.	Every failure has a lesson and an opportunity for improvement.

EMOTIONAL INTELLIGENCE: IN ACTION

The following few questions will help you to reflect on EI.

Self-Awareness is where you should begin to work.

- Take feedback from your leader and two other people around you on

  › How you come across with respect to your ability to handle emotions?

  › Do you understand other's emotions?

- Reflect on your emotions a couple of times in a day and ask yourself—How are you feeling?

- Reflect on how you feel and how you react

  › When people criticize you?

  › When you hear bad feedback?

  › When there are difficult conversations?

- Observe the pattern—What comes out from your reflection and feedback?

- Choose a difficult situation to work on and in that situation

  › Breathe deeper

  › Notice what you feel

  › How can you take charge of how do you want to feel?

  › Pause before responding

- Practice, Practice and Practice.

75% of careers are derailed for reasons related to emotional competencies, including inability to handle interpersonal problems; unsatisfactory team leadership during times of difficulty or conflict; or inability to adapt to change or elicit trust.

The Center for Creative Leadership

REFERENCES

1. CareerBuilder. *Seventy-one percent of employers say they value emotional intelligence over IQ, According to CareerBuilder survey.* Available from: https://www.careerbuilder.com/share/aboutus/pressreleasesdetail. aspx?id=pr652&sd=8/18/2011&ed=08/18/2011 [Accessed 14 February 2020].

2. Rode JC, Arthaud-Day M, Ramaswami A, Howes S. A time-lagged study of emotional intelligence and salary. *Journal of Vocational Behavior.* 2017;101: 77–89.

3. Study.com. *Four quadrant model for emotional intelligence for supervisors.* Available from: https://study.com/academy/lesson/four-quadrant-model-for-emotional-intelligence-for-supervisors.html [Accessed 14 February 2020].

4. Goleman D. What makes a leader. *Harvard Business Review.* Available from: http://athena.ecs.csus.edu/~buckley/CSc233/ What-makes-a-Leader-HBR.pdf [Accessed 14 February 2020].

13

FIVE BLIND SPOTS THAT MAY HOLD YOU BACK

❝ ❞

The greatest deception men suffer is from their own opinions.

LEONARDO DA VINCI

I am glad that you have gone through the stories of 10 successful leaders and have reached up to this point. I hope that each story has given you some food for thought and that you have picked up a few ideas that can help you achieve growth. While it is very important to add new tools to your arsenal, it is equally important to be vary of some of the things that you should avoid.

A blind spot is an unconscious behaviour of yours which is quite obvious to others and oblivious to yourself. While you may complement your performance with additional skills you gain from the experience of other leaders, success may still elude you as each of the blind spots has the potential to pull you down. This chapter lists the five common blind spots that may stop you from your next promotion.

KNOW IT ALL

Keep learning; don't be arrogant by assuming that you know it all, that you have a monopoly on the truth; always assume that you can learn something from someone else.

Jack Welch

Success makes you prone to this blind spot. If you have been successful in the past by using a strategy that you developed, you continue to use that even when the situation changes and the relevance of the same reduces. When others try to suggest some changes, you quote your successes and challenge them.

A few leaders may feel that they know the best way to do things. They may also think that the leaders are expected to know it all and have the fear that if anybody else has a better idea, then they will be a failure and lose their position. They work hard to keep the illusion of knowing all, as they do not want to fail. They stop listening to other people who may be smarter, and this blind spot makes them stagnate.

On the other hand, reality is that many amazing leaders in the world are aware that they do not know it all, rather they surround themselves with people who challenge their thinking. They look for improvement all the time and are open to listen to anyone.

If you have this blind spot, some of the behaviours you could recognize it by are given below:

- You feel insecure when others have better ideas. You would not want to acknowledge great ideas given by others in front of a group.

- You downplay better ideas given by others or feel that you need to add to that idea to make it better.

- When your peers have a meeting and you are not there, you fear that you may miss knowing the information.

- When your team tries to share alternate ideas, you get irritated and push harder. You let them know that you are in charge.

NEED TO CONTROL

Those who like to command and control others are always scared of their authority been challenged or criticized.

Ifeanyi Enoch Onuoha

Perfectionism makes you prone to this blind spot. You feel the need to be in complete control and try to dictate each step. In fact, you treat your team as a tool to multiply your own self and try to make each one think and act like you.

The truth is that when you control things a bit too tightly, you tend to lose the ability of your team to function in a productive and innovative way. They become less passionate about the work, because they are not able to contribute with their heart and mind, they are just using their head and hands to follow your instructions. You have to let them be, you have to trust them to meet your expectations. You must have the patience for them to gain that confidence and start producing great results. The better they become, the more you can achieve as a team and the lesser the pressure of responsibility on you. You should invest in their growth and you must develop them such that they surpass your abilities. When your team grows, you will grow with the team.

If you have this blind spot, some of the behaviours you could recognize it by are given below:

- You are usually not satisfied with the work of your team members.

- You often feel frustrated because your team members do not go about the task as efficiently as yourself.

- You jump into details and look for problems and mistakes to highlight, rather than appreciating the good elements.

- You need to know where all your team members are and what they are doing.

- You ask for updates too often.

- You prefer to be copied on all communication.

- You delay decisions.

- You are overwhelmed with work.

CHANGE MAY NOT BE GOOD

What the human being is best at doing is interpreting all new information so that their prior conclusions remain intact.

Warren Buffet

Fear and inflexibility make you prone to this blind spot. You get comfortable with the way of doing things. You are afraid that changing things may bring out new unknowns. Incremental changes do not appeal to you and you believe that the cost of change is more than the benefit of the change. When others suggest changes, you question their motives and wonder what they might gain from the change. You strongly believe that if something needs to change, it must not be you, it should be the other people who should change. You believe you are doing your best and want others to step up their efforts to align with you.

The truth is that change is very natural and if you do not change along with the environment, taking small steps at a time, you will soon be out of sync with the whole system and become less relevant. You will then need to make a big change just to fit in and that will be very difficult. This is one key reason that many professionals find themselves on the plateau, as they fail to change and acquire new skills or capabilities necessary to stay relevant. When looking at the small changes, you must judge their value through their alignment with the long-term trends. If the change prepares you for the future, be ready to adopt it.

If you have this blind spot, some of the behaviours you could recognize it by are given below:

- You are still doing the same things you did last year, and exactly the same way.

- You have not added any skill to yourself in last six months.

- When confronted with data, you propose to have a re-look, delaying any decision to change.

- You believe that once we have a great way of doing things, there is no need to look for a new one.

- You are too busy solving today's problems that you do not look into the need to change for future. You do not have time for it.

- You fear that the change is going to affect you negatively.

BLAMING OTHERS OR CIRCUMSTANCES

The absence of evidence is not evidence of absence.

Carl Sagan

Overconfidence and certain fears make you prone to this blind spot. In your overconfidence, you tend to ignore your own role and blame everyone else in any problem situation or for any failure. You feel lesser need for introspection or self-awareness, and you look for faults elsewhere. You strongly believe that you cannot do wrong and always work in the interest of the organization.

Self-awareness is one of the biggest strengths of a leader, and a leader must know that he/she cannot be the best in everything. When something goes wrong, they must look at their own self first. They should realize that blaming circumstances is not going to help them succeed, and that they need to change to align themselves with new circumstances to continue to assure their own success.

If you have this blind spot, some of the behaviours you could recognize it by are given below:

- You have not taken responsibility of any failure, but you have always found the person in the team responsible for the problem.

- You have in the last one year come out with many corrective measures that others must take and so far, you have had no reason to change.

- Sometimes you feel helpless in the light of failures because there is nothing you could have done to prevent them.

- You fear to ask for other's suggestions and feedback.

- Before having a discussion to understand the issue a little better, you have decided whom to blame.

- You fear collaboration.

LISTENING SELECTIVELY

Leaders who don't listen will eventually be surrounded by people who have nothing to say.

Andy Stanley

Preconceived notions of success can lead to this blind spot. You have decided what you are going to do irrespective of what others believe. So, when you talk to them, you listen to only those pieces that align with your thinking. You are the one who is doing most of the talking all the time because you do not believe others can add much value. When others say something, which does not match with your understanding of the situation, you tend to listen to respond and not listen to understand.

If you are not open to new ideas and thoughts, you are most likely headed to the plateau. Sooner or later you will run out of your own ideas and abilities. Listening to others and co-creating ideas and solutions can ensure that you are not alone and that you have the power of the whole team with you. You need to believe that others have equal interest in the success of the organization and that you do not have to be fixated on your own solutions. The power of the dialogue is in finding new solutions that you did not think yourself.

If you have this blind spot, some of the behaviours you could recognize it by are given below:

- You do not pay attention to the speaker if it does not align with your thinking.

- You are more concerned about how things are said, rather than what is being said.

- You are thinking about how you are going to respond while the other person is still talking.

- You interrupt them again and again challenging at every step.

- You know something is wrong but do not voice your opinion because you want to avoid conflict.

- You avoid eye contact when the other person is talking.

WORKING ON YOUR BLIND SPOTS

The main challenge with a blind spot is that you are not aware of what you are missing on. No one is perfect but becoming more aware of your blind spots will certainly help you to enhance your chances for success. The following two things are crucial for understanding your blind spots.

- Self-awareness

- Feedback

I hope that the few pointers provided here will help you identify any blind spots. Then you must make conscious effort to avoid them, a coach or a mentor can help you come with a plan and help you realize your potential.

14

THE UNWRITTEN RULES OF PROMOTION

Not all the rules for your next promotion may be clear. Some not even relate to the subject matter expertise or specific skill sets. They may link to the softer parts that collectively build your personality and forge a perception about yourself within the organization. But be aware that for decision-makers, these rules make perfect sense and they allow them to take a call on whether you can succeed at senior levels or not.

Almost everyone progresses to Stage 3 (Contributing through Others) but not many exit this stage with upward growth into Stage 4 (Contributing Strategically). Promotion is more about your potential and promise of a future that you can help create. If you believe you are a 'high-potential', I am sure you are being considered. Many seek the coveted spot but only one among them, who is 'the best among equals' will get it. You may have to work on certain aspects to improve your chances. You may have to change the way you do things today and it may not be easy. It will take time and consistent efforts. If you keep at it and look for ways to complement your present strengths, the payoffs can be huge. Get ready to step outside the comfort zone and start.

Whenever the stakes are high and only one among many can be the winner, everything counts. It is not just about that final decision point of choosing between one among many, it is about the complete journey of an individual. That is the reason that this book talks about 10 different facets that you can explore. You can use them to complement the strengths you already have, to forge a new path and to overcome the hurdle of the 'plateau'. You have the opportunity today to create your own future.

THE SUPER 10

Accelerate Your Journey to the Next Promotion

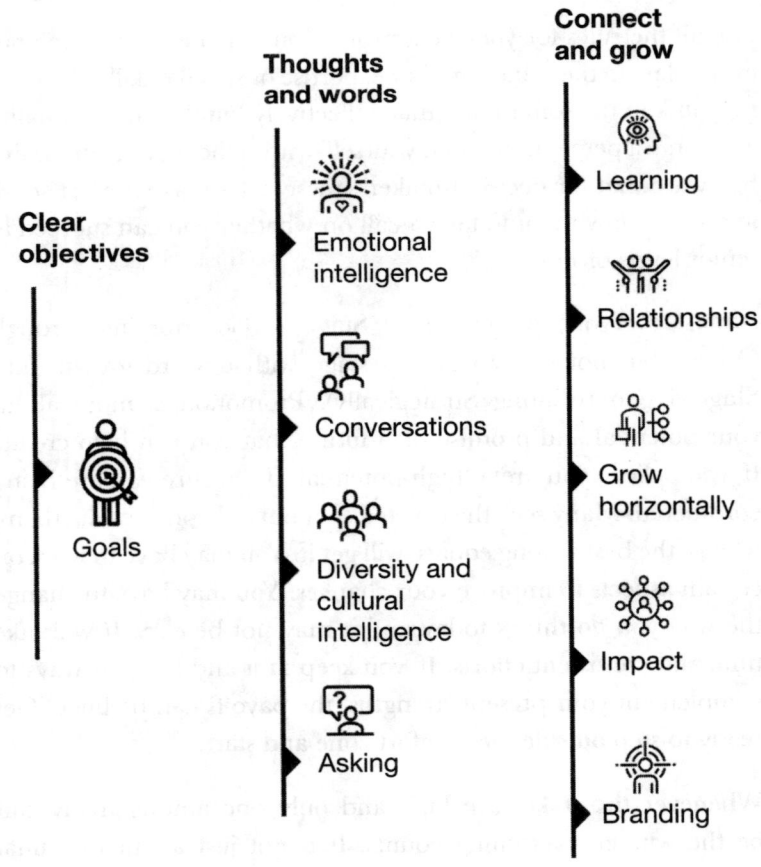

Each of the 10 facets augments your chances at success. To help you choose your priorities, you may consider the high-level impact of each of the facets as follows.

When you are compared with others, your technical ability or domain knowledge will most likely be considered first. You are required to know your own domain with some level of expertise and as R. Mahalakshmi says, you need to continue to augment your skills by continuing to learn. You must focus on your strengths as well as skills you need for your future roles. You should make your learning and development plans and execute well. Seek a mentor who can guide you on the path.

Not only should you be great at your domain, you must also be acknowledged for it, within your organization, industry and beyond. As Malur Narayan says that your personal brand should be aligned with the role that you seek. As organizations and business environments continue to change fast, you must focus on what role you want to play and work hard to create a space for yourself.

Leaders are expected to create impact beyond boundaries and that cannot happen without the collaboration and a cross domain knowledge and understanding. As Dr Tapan Sahoo says, you must focus on developing core strengths and then invest time and energy to understand adjacent areas. To create such an impact, you must understand the big picture.

You must develop the breadth of knowledge to create such an impact. Almost all the seniors level roles are multi domain. You should endeavour to gain experience across domains on your way up to the top roles. As Arindam says, being on the plateau is not bad in itself, it gives you a great perspective of where you are and where you want to go. You must choose to step off this temporary height to start climbing the next one. This will mean actively seeking diverse roles and for many, this may even mean working across industries too.

You will also need the ability to connect with people at all levels and take them along. This will require you to have a highly developed EI ability. As Amandeep Gupta says, professional competencies are just like having a passport, necessary but not sufficient. EI is like the visa that completes the requirements for success.

Sometimes, the roles will go beyond geographies and you will encounter new levels of diversity. Your ability to leverage the diversity to create a competitive advantage for your organization is equally important. As Ashley Passow says that once you start working with executives, your ability to get the support from a diverse set of experts counts a lot. You must be able to connect various diverse teams together and make them work towards one goal.

One cannot achieve cooperation without having the ability to have effective conversations. As Steve Alexander says, advancement of the ranks often leads to dealing with more and more ambiguity. The ability to use conversations to turn ambiguity into understanding and then using the understanding to solve larger problems at work becomes extremely important. At senior levels, you should have the ability to simplify the complex stuff to make meaningful conversations across a wide spectrum of experts.

Many great conversations may still not get you what you want unless you can be specific and ask for what you desire. As Apurva Purohit says, before you table your ask, you must introspect and be sure that you are ready. It pays to spend the effort in preparing for these crucial conversations which can result in great benefits for you.

To have great conversations, the leader must be able to build lasting relationships. As Kulmeet Bawa says, such relationships can only be forged through genuine interest. He wants you to really care about your people and your organization and serve with passion and authenticity. He says that once you connect with people in the right way, all other things start automatically falling in the right place.

Finally, no progress in possible on any of the fronts unless you have a goal and stay focused to achieve it. As Ravinder Dang says that if you are serious about your goal, you will make regular and consistent progress towards it each day. He believes that you must find work that aligns with your core values and work passionately. It is impossible to fake passion, and lack of it leads to mediocre outcomes. Ravinder also says that you do not need to be perfect. Seek feedback, acknowledge your growth areas and keep working.

PATH AHEAD

Depending on where you are in your career and what strengths you have already developed, it will be prudent to choose a couple of development areas and start working on them. Monitor your progress regularly. Once you are comfortable, pick up the next and start working on it. All these areas are interrelated and working on one will help you make progress against some others.

Ready to realize your dreams?

ABOUT THE AUTHOR

Manbir is an Executive and Leadership Coach (Professional Certificated Coach, PCC-ICF). She is also a Conversational Intelligence (C-IQ) Enhanced Skills Practitioner and a key-note speaker.

She specializes in coaching leaders from technology organizations. Manbir helps leaders and entrepreneurs to align themselves and their teams to the strategic goals, unleash their own and their team's potential. Over years, she has developed specific frameworks to help organizations and leaders achieve success in the most effective way. Her frameworks make coaching progress measurable and she believes in creating value for her clients in every engagement. Her clients include executives from various technology companies from India, UK, USA, Middle East and so on.

She is also the author of the book *Are You The Leader You Want To Be?* Her book combines various principles, studies and practices to present a path-breaking, five-part framework called HUMAN which helps engage your teams in a human way. The book presents a business story-based narrative, which has been very well received by the readers. This book was nominated as top 5 Business Books in India for *BBLF CK Prahalad Best Business Book Award 2019.*

Manbir has more than two decades of work experience. Prior to being a coach, Manbir has worked in the corporate world for various Indian and multinational IT companies in roles such as development, operations, presales, people management and consulting. This work experience enables her to relate to her clients in a more immersive way.

Her professional goals are aimed at helping millions of leaders and teams across the world to develop the abilities to break the shackles that may hold them back and help them achieve their potential. As new changes in the business and personal worlds affect the individuals, she takes a step back to study, research, reflect and come up with simple methods that can help professionals from all spheres to continue to excel despite these changes. She writes articles, blogs and books to share the hard-earned wisdom, lessons learned and simple-yet-effective frameworks with all.

On a personal front, she is quite dedicated to her family. She believes in fostering deeper connections. She works hard but always makes space for the people who make the sun shine in her world. She believes in work–life integration and has achieved that elusive balance that we all seek. In her spare time, she pursues hobbies such as theatre, dance and poetry.

You can connect to her using her website http://manbirkaur.com to stay updated on the latest articles via her blog, follow her on Facebook via https://www.facebook.com/BuzzManbir/, Twitter @BuzzManbir, Instagram @BuzzManbir.